With Gissing in Italy

With Gissing in Italy

The Memoirs of Brian Ború Dunne

Paul F. Mattheisen • *Arthur C. Young*
Pierre Coustillas
EDITORS

Ohio University Press
ATHENS

Ohio University Press, Athens, Ohio 45701
© 1999 by Brian B. Dunne II
Introduction and Notes © 1999 by
Paul F. Mattheisen, Arthur C. Young, and
Pierre Coustillas

Printed in the United States of America
Ohio University Press books are printed on acid-free paper ∞ ™
03 02 01 00 99   5 4 3 2 1

Frontispiece: Brian Ború Dunne in Rome, 1898 (B. B. Dunne II).

Book design by Chiquita Babb

Library of Congress Cataloging-in-Publication Data
Dunne, Brian Ború.
    With Gissing in Italy : the memoirs of Brian Ború Dunne / Paul F.
Mattheisen, Arthur C. Young, Pierre Coustillas, editors.
        p.   cm.
    Includes bibliographical references and index.
    ISBN 0-8214-1258-2 (alk. paper)
    1. Gissing, George, 1857–1903—Journeys—Italy—Rome. 2. Gissing,
George, 1857–1903—Friends and associates. 3. Rome (Italy)—Social
life and customs—19th century. 4. Rome (Italy)—Intellectual
life—19th century. 5. Novelists, English—19th century—Biography.
6. Americans—Italy—Rome—History—19th century. 7. British—
Italy—Rome—History—19th century. 8. Journalists—United States—
Biography. 9. Dunne, Brian Ború. I. Mattheisen, Paul F.
II. Young, Arthur C. III. Coustillas, Pierre. IV. Title.
PR4717.D86   1999
828'.803—dc21   98-50127
    [b]   CIP

CONTENTS

ILLUSTRATIONS

The Via del Boschetto in Rome, where Gissing lived in 1898, as it appears today

No. 3 Piazza di Spagna, Rome, where Gissing paid visits to Alfred Lambart

Facing page 191

Mark Twain's note to Dunne, showing that the beginning of the "Sentiment" was cut off from the page

ACKNOWLEDGMENTS

For permission to publish the memoirs of BrianBorú Dunne we are indebted to the writer's son, Brian B. Dunne II, of La Jolla, California. Permission to publish letters to the writer has been granted by The Society of Authors on behalf of the Bernard Shaw Estate; by A. P. Watt on behalf of the H. G. Wells Estate; by Robert H. Hirst, General Editor of the Mark Twain Project at U. S. C. Berkeley, California; and by the Archdiocese of Baltimore on behalf of Cardinal Gibbons.

Mr. Richard H. Christmas, Mayor of St. Leo and nephew of Frederic J. Dunne, has been generous with his time in searching out and lending us documents relating to the genealogy of the Dunne family. For their important help in the documentation we are grateful to Dr. Francesco Badolato; Hélène Coustillas; Prince Guillaume de Croÿ; F. Demeure Delespaul; Dr. Marysa Demoor; Maria Dimitriadou; Robert H. Hirst; Dr. James Horgan, historian of St. Leo College; John Huffman, of the Mark Twain Research Foundation; Françoise Leleu-Tayara, Librarian at the University of Lille; Photothèque Boutique-Grard, Musée de Douai; Christiane Piérard, Librarian, Mons; Gene K. Rinkel, director of Special Collections, University of Illinois; Joan Rogers, Water Clerk of San Antonio, Florida; Padre Giovanni Rulli; Domenico Russo; Patrick Vanleene; and Christophe Taquin, *échevin de la culture*, Mons.

With Gissing in Italy

Introduction

GISSING SCHOLARS first encountered the name of Brian
Ború Dunne in Royal Gettmann's 1959 edition of the correspondence between Gissing and H. G. Wells, where it appears in an an-
notation to the letter of December 8, 1896. In the letter, Gissing
explained to Wells his need to impose limits on his sociability: "The
Omar is the only club I belong to, of any kind, and I simply dare
not go in for more conviviality. The fact is, I enjoy it too much, and
could easily become a mere haunter of taverns." There seems to be
nothing extraordinary about Gissing's comment. We know he greatly
valued his association with the celebrated Omar Khayyám Club,
where he met so many important literary people, and we know
that he had precious little time to dissipate his energies in frivolity.
And yet when Gettmann annotated the correspondence he feared
that "at first glance this statement may seem to be out of character,"
and found it necessary to establish Gissing's capacity for such conviviality by adducing two quotations to support it.

The first was from Wells himself, who in his *Experiment in Autobiography* (1934) declared that Gissing "craved to laugh, jest, enjoy,
stride along against the wind, shout, 'quaff mighty flagons'" (p. 38).
There is nothing surprising here either. Wells had known Gissing
since the Omar Khayyám Club dinner of November 20, 1896, and
he spoke on his own authority. But the other quotation was from a

letter to Wells from Brian Ború Dunne: "I look upon Gissing as one of the most cheerful, luxury-loving, witty people I have ever met." There, indeed, is a Gissing who is out of character.

In the Gissing/Wells correspondence, Dunne was then an unknown quantity, identified as a young American who met Gissing in Italy in 1898 (actually 1897) and saw him frequently in Rome. Yet his comment appears to be so extraordinary that we may wonder on what real authority he could make such a pronouncement. Gettmann thought so too, for he tracked him down in Santa Fe, wrote to him, and later thanked him for lending out his memoir of Gissing—the first indication that such a memoir existed. But Gettmann made little use of it in his edition, leaving us with a passage by Gissing and two quite different commentaries on it. Yet Gissing's own meaning seems to be clear, and even if we can sense a slight exaggeration in his expression of it, we may attribute that to the kind of epistolary ebullience he adopted to avoid giving the impression that he had become an unsociable recluse. Gissing at this time, being embroiled in the most difficult domestic troubles, was frantically trying to earn money with a succession of short stories and was becoming even more fully immersed in the world of editors, publishers, and literary figures. If he were to fritter away his time in the congeniality of club life he would simply dispel the energies needed to survive. For this reason, too, we accept Wells's comment, especially if we remember Gissing's exuberant early days and allow that in his later life, no matter how much he might "crave" those things which Wells named, he was too often beset by wretched circumstances to indulge that side of his nature. Besides, Gissing was supremely delighted at having met Wells, whom he called unreservedly "the friend of a lifetime," and it was in the company of Wells that he most often found the opportunity of unrestrained joy.

It is significant that Dunne's comment is from the letter he wrote to Wells in 1933, very close to the time Wells was working on his autobiography, with its long section on Gissing, and just prior to the time when Dunne himself was moved to write a memoir of his friend. But Wells spoke more of a yearning and an inclination than of an achievement and a habit, and Dunne's view would have astonished nearly everyone who had known Gissing during his lifetime—or, indeed, nearly anyone who wrote of him then or at any later time. Even when Gissing was at the height of his reputation as one of England's three leading novelists, it was commonly thought that the reason his novels did not sell widely was that the general public did not care to read such tales of misery, and it was known to his friends and assumed by others that many of these stories reflected the immense misery of his own life. Later, when Gissing's private life became more publicly known, very few persons even then appeared to claim that he was either witty or cheerful, and certainly there was little evidence that Gissing could ever have afforded a life of luxury even if he had wanted it. Any hints that the pervasive oppression of Gissing's life might have been alleviated by occasional periods of cheerfulness were submerged under the prevailing view of his wretchedness. And indeed, if we read Dunne's seemingly exaggerated comment in the context of the paragraph from which it was quoted, it seems clear that Dunne himself, having read the family edition of the letters in 1927, was by then somewhat aware of this sordid side of Gissing's life. In the same letter in which he told Wells that he regarded Gissing as cheerful, he added: "But he may have led a hell of a life. I read his *Letters*. Pretty dull stuff."

Much of this and more, of course, was known to Wells, who wrote from the perspective of a longer friendship, but clearly if Dunne were to have written a memoir of Gissing even then, it would be quite different from what we read of him in Wells's book. It would be quite as authentic as—and even perhaps more genuine than—the contrived reflections of Wells, who sometimes saw Gissing through a darker glass of his own. But it would reflect solely the happier months Dunne spent with Gissing in Italy, a point it is necessary to stress. In the event, Dunne's recorded recollections are far more spontaneous. Untainted by any cosmic view, he wrote of Gissing's daily life in a way no one else has done, and retrieved for us a unique aspect of Gissing's happiest period, when he seems

actually to have become "cheerful," "witty," and even "luxury-loving."
To explain this it will be helpful to review the conditions under
which Gissing fled to Italy, and then to reflect on his encounter with
this young American, on Dunne's own life and background, on the
friendship that developed between these very different personalities, and on Dunne's later approach to the writing of a memoir of
his English friend who had introduced him to H. G. Wells. To understand a memoir, we must also understand the person who wrote it.

As early as March 3, 1896, Gissing defined for his brother
Algernon one of the ironic paradoxes of his life at the time: "My
public progress is terribly balanced by private misfortunes & miseries." Ultimately it was the private miseries which drove him to
Italy, but by public progress he meant his professional success, which
had been rising rapidly since the beginning of 1895, but which now,
in another irony, demanded of him a busy schedule of professional
and social obligations that could threaten to absorb his time at the
cost of his work. It was during this period that his friend Henry
Norman, literary editor of the *Daily Chronicle,* publicly recognized
him, along with Hardy and Meredith, as one of England's three
foremost novelists, and his work was in demand by editors and
publishers—the kind of literary success that was thrusting him into
a social life to which he was unaccustomed. On that occasion (July
13, 1895), as the guest of Clement King Shorter, he was introduced
to the Omar Khayyám Club at a celebrated meeting in which he
(among others) gave a speech in honor of George Meredith, renewed his acquaintance with Hardy, then wrote to Clara Collet of
his enjoyment in meeting and talking with such figures as Edward
Clodd, Louis F. Austin, Henry Norman, and William Sharp, also
commenting in his diary on Arthur Wing Pinero and Moncure
Conway. On other occasions he amused Wilfrid Meynell, and
William Massingham wanted him to play golf. For the first time he
was also invited to one of Edward Clodd's famous Whitsuntide
weekend parties at his Aldeburgh seaside home, where at some
point Clodd entertained nearly all the important men of the time,
this particular weekend including Sir Benjamin Ward Richardson,

Clement King Shorter, George Whale, L. F. Austin and Grant Allen.

These, of course, are just some of the formal gatherings. His letters and the diary show that Gissing was also seeing more of his old friends, meeting with editors, publishers, agents, and other literary men. A brief sample of the names will help remind us of the nature and the extent of his social life. In June of 1896, for instance, he met J. M. Barrie, Maarten Maartens, and Harold Frederic at an Omar dinner, on his return home visited W. H. Hudson, met Justin McCarthy, Israel Zangwill, Andrew Lang, and Nisbet Bain at a *Cosmopolis* dinner given by its editor Felix Ortmans, spent time with the Travers family, who had befriended him, and once in the diary recorded the result of this frantic activity—"utterly wasting my time now." In July he lunched with Edmund Gosse, along with Austin Dobson, Andrew Lang, and Hamo Thornycroft, and later called upon Colles, his agent, and Bullen, his publisher, dined with C. F. Keary, spent an overnight with Clodd, and with John Davidson went to another Omar dinner, the one at which he first met H. G. Wells. He was also visiting with such old friends as George Meredith and Thomas Hardy, Henry Hick and Morley Roberts.

Doubtless there was an immensely pleasurable side to this increasingly frenetic social activity, but in spite of the varied range of his activities, Gissing viewed it all as part of his attempt to further his career, to increase the demand for his work and so earn more by it—as he wrote to Clara Collet: "Be assured that all my social pleasures are hard matters of business." Perhaps owing to his increasing troubles and responsibilities, to his growing sense of professional success, and doubtless also to his apprehension of the future, Gissing was more than ever determined to make money at this time. By the end of 1895 he realized that he could make as much as £500 a year, and was so concerned about his son Walter's life and education that he began to hope he could set aside £1000 for his education. But the birth of his second son in January 1896 added to his responsibilities, and by 1897 he was acutely aware of the crushing expense in maintaining what he called "three directions of steady payment—Walter at Wakefield—Epsom [his wife, Edith, and son Alfred]—& here."

One reason Gissing could enhance his income during these years, and even hope to put something aside for Walter's education, was that he had turned to the more profitable medium of the short story—and then to the two short novels, *Sleeping Fires* and *The Paying Guest,* which he did not count among his serious works. Editors were clamoring for his work, and he churned out stories accordingly, but he very well knew that all of this kept him from his serious writing—as he wrote to Eduard Bertz in August of 1895, "It is now a year since I finished my last novel. . . . I have a lot of stories to write for the *English Illustrated,* & other editors are constantly demanding that kind of thing. But I must close my ears." His financial needs continued, however, and in the midst of domestic turmoil he confessed to Clara Collet that his "first duty is to make money." When he was able in April of 1896 to send Walter to the school run by his sisters in Wakefield and so to begin work on *The Whirlpool,* he wrote to Collet (May 24) that he was at last "recovering my self-respect," and was even able once again to "have the joy of moulding phrases"—what he called deliberate, "steady work," not the "hurried, money-earning" kind. Yet three months later he told Roberts "It begins to be a question whether I shall ever again finish a book, interruptions are so frequent & so serious," and that there was "nothing to do but to labour for an income." In August of 1896, a spiritual and practical low point, he told Bertz his labors were affecting even the quality of his work: "Two months ago I wrote a miserable short story for 'Cosmopolis,' & repented as soon as I had sent it; but the price was £20, & I could not afford to lose the money."

Gissing finished *The Whirlpool* on December 18, 1896; on the following January 11 he got "a good idea for a short novel," and then wrote to Algernon that he had been asked—and had "half promised" —to write a monograph on Dickens, "the length of Macmillan's Statesmen series." This was to be an important event in the months leading to his flight to Italy. It would, he said, be "a new effort for me," but he added that "such an engagement is very perilous, considering that I can never count on a week's quietness." What he meant by this was not only the interruptions caused by his social life and by the painful effort to produce short stories, but also the constant rages and fulminations of his wife, Edith, which, more than anything else in these years, eventually put him into such a sustained depression that it is a wonder he did any work at all. One of the most curious things about this tumultuous domestic relationship is that Gissing kept very little record of it in his diary. The few notations there are simple and unspecified, such as: "A time of great domestic misery." But on September 4, 1895, we find some indication as to why he was so curt and so unspecific: "Infinite domestic misery going on from day to day. I keep as silent as possible." It is this silence in response to Edith which also permeates the diary, where, however, we find a decisive clue in the entry of October 3, 1895. There he says that he "Wrote to Miss Orme, and to Miss Collet," the two women who had recently befriended him and were always willing to give him whatever help they could. With these two, Gissing had until then kept equally silent about his household affairs and his troubles with Edith, but now in his letter to Clara Collet he disemburdened himself so frankly and so fully as to alter their relationship considerably. It was a decisive move, essentially a kind of preliminary to the final break with Edith, the disposal of his children, and the escape into Italy.

By writing to Clara Collet in this way, Gissing was not only drawing her far more intimately into his affairs, but also giving us an insight into how his domestic troubles were affecting his work, his outlook, and his health, mental and physical. He was, he said, "battling for life against deathly tendencies," explaining that he had patiently endured being shut up at home for four years "out of regard for Edith," that his "social pleasures" were "hard matters of business" and that he had kept them strictly within narrow limits. "Utterly unmerited abuse, slander, obstruction—day after day, year after year," he said, "has worked its natural effect." It is important to stress that in his writing as well as his social activities Gissing was continually having to overcome the devastating misery of his domestic life, the alternating rages and sullenness of Edith, her scorn, her railings, her treatment of Walter, and her jealousy of his work. He saw that the downward spiral must be changed radically: "What I have to do is to work & earn money; Edith's part is to see that I am not encumbered with needless vexations."

Through such letters as this we can understand better the impediments underlying his efforts to make something of his new professional standing. Even in his other correspondence we can see how all this was increasing his anxiety, giving him an attitude of hopeless desperation and—most importantly—an increasing sense that the end was near, that he was approaching the final stages of his life. At a time when Gissing was at the seashore trying to enjoy a vacation with his son Walter, he confessed that he was having very little pleasure: "Indeed, every year I feel a most appreciable decline in my powers of enjoyment. Nothing gives me very much pleasure now-a-days, & I look forward to a time of very dreary impassivity." In the same letter to Bertz of August 3, 1896, he wrote of his "illness & depression & consequent inability to bring myself to anything at all—a curious nullification of the will. . . ." If it seems incredible that Gissing, or any writer, could continue to produce any work at all under such circumstances, even just to keep alive, it is surely a degree of heroism that could keep him thinking still of "the joy of moulding phrases," the pleasure in writing the kind of serious literature for which he had earned his high reputation.

Writing to Morley Roberts a month later, he was again troubled by the impediments to his work, and this, of course, exacerbated his money problems: "There is nothing to do but labour for an income, with the slight hope of securing just a little more than must be spent from day to day." More significant here, however, is the evidence of his mental condition and his view of the future: "I have entered upon the last stage of life's journey, & can hope for no more cheery excursions from the beaten track." It is doubtless in part this frame of mind that later drove him to his "cheery excursion" into Italy, but his yearning for such an event is suggested even a year earlier in a postscript he added to a letter to Clara Collet: "Shorter is in Rome —think of it!"

By early 1897 it was increasingly clear that a crisis was at hand. On February 5 Gissing entered into the diary the prophetic comment "Misery in house," and a few days later he wrote to Collet, "I am near despair. No hope of any writing—one might as well sit down to work in a mad-house." He had been working on the story that was to become *The Town Traveller,* and on February 9 he noted that things were still not going well: "Fine. Story again out of gear. New scheme." Then came the critical moment of his final break with Edith, and there is a corresponding break in the diary from that day until June 2, when he wrote a summary entry for the previous months. We can, however, more or less trace his movements from the letters. On February 10 he wrote to Clara Collet: "I am driven from home with outrageous insults, & shall never return." Gissing's health had been of some concern to him since December of 1896, when, unable to shake a dangerous cough he had contracted in August, he went to see Dr. Beaumont, who "says there is a weak point in right lung. This may be a grave matter, and may not." Now, just having been driven from home, he went immediately to his friend, Dr. Henry Hick. Hick was, as he said, "much graver than Beaumont, and talks about a 6-months' voyage," but he also insisted that he see a lung specialist. Three days later, on February 16, Dr. Pye-Smith found "a decided weakness in one lung," and commanded him to go at once to South Devon, thereby condemning him to an exile at Budleigh Salterton until he returned on May 31. His health had now become another decisive factor in the months before his flight to Rome. Without any diary entries to consult, it is especially difficult to keep track of the fluctuations in his condition during this period. His letters are peppered with allusions to his health, but Gissing habitually tailored his letters to suit the correspondent, and the descriptions of his physical condition at this time necessarily depended on the recipient. At Budleigh Salterton he seemed at first to improve, but his condition was so variable and his descriptions of it so general that it is perhaps safest to rely on his own assessment in writing to Morley Roberts that he was neither better nor worse. On April 16 he told Bertz that, although he was better in health, and his cough was less troublesome, still "I cannot climb a hill without terrible shortness of breath." During May a new phrase that enters his letters is repeated enough to become something of a refrain. On May 1 he reported to Colles that he would turn in a story "if I live long enough." To Collet on the eleventh he said he would think of her "ten years hence, if I live. . . ." And again on the thirtieth he told her that he would reprint in a new edition of *The Whirlpool* some lines from a review of it "If I live long enough."

Gissing was not able to write much at Budleigh Salterton, but for a time he was still able to read widely for his Dickens book. Once again, it is hard to trace his progress because for three months he kept no diary and wrote fewer letters than usual. When he told Algernon on January 23 of having accepted the Dickens proposal, he hoped to finish the book before he took his holiday, and told Clara Collet that "All sorts of thoughts are coming to me for the Dickens book." At the end of February he asked her to buy two of Dickens's novels so that he could scribble notes on them, and in March he was telling her that his admiration for Dickens was increasing, asking her to send him more of the novels. Still, he wrote to Algernon that "life is a great burden," and a few days later: "My one consolation is, that the greater part of life is struggled through —past & over." On April 11 he told Collet that he had done no writing at all, explained the arrangements that were being made for Edith and Alfred, and said, "I am too sick of life to write about anything else." Five days later, in a letter to Bertz, he used another phrase which threatened to become a refrain: "I fear the best of life is over." His loneliness was somewhat relieved by visits, first from his son Walter for a fortnight, and then for another fortnight from the Wellses, but writing was still impossible. He continued reading his books on the sixth century, in preparation for his final effort, the historical novel *Veranilda*. And then suddenly, once back in Epsom, he brought himself to begin the writing of *The Town Traveller*, the book that was to bring him £350 for five weeks' work, having told Clara Collet on May 21 that "Dickens (if I do it at all) must wait."

On September 6 Gissing aroused Edith's "fury and insult" by announcing that he intended to go to Italy, and four days later Eliza Orme undertook to find rooms for her and Alfred, a step which would allow him more easily to remove himself from that source of grief. It was a sudden announcement, but as early as August 18 he had written to Herbert Sturmer that "I have been seriously meditating a flight to Italy." Flight was exactly the word to describe his escape from the responsibilities at home and his yearning for the ancient country of glorious achievement. "The familiar land," he said, "beckons me as I lie awake at night." The Dickens was occasionally still on his mind, as when he wrote to Algernon on August 12 that the book was "to be done by Xmas," but eventually Italy and Dickens came together in his head, and on August 28 he told Algernon that he had decided to go "to the shores of the Mediterranean," and that "I shall write my Dickens book at Florence—a place which does not excite me, & where there are good libraries." Significantly, here he first mentions his plan to get materials for another book, which had apparently been in his mind, and which was to become *By the Ionian Sea*. It seems that the drive for Italy was not an altogether impromptu one, and that the justification for it was intimately connected with his future as a writer. He had gained his stature as a novelist, the *Dickens* was to prove himself as a critic, and the travel book, for which he needed Italy, was to establish himself in yet another departure from the novel. It is clear that he was already adumbrating the *Private Papers of Henry Ryecroft* as a fitting "farewell" to his career as a writer, and the historical novel was to be a final proof of his achievement as both a novelist and a superb classical scholar. Whether he knew it clearly or not, it seems that the end of his life was not altogether outside of his plan. Later, even Dunne noticed it in Rome: Gissing's recognition that "Life is drawing to a close" is listed as a topic for the memoir.

In a letter he wrote to Hick two days after his letter to Algernon, Florence had become Siena, and he said that he had "some hard reading to get thro'" before going there. To Algernon on September 4 he wrote that he was "toiling at my Dickens, so as not to have to take many books," and it is clear that even if he was not yet writing, he was planning it out in some detail. And by this time his enthusiasm and confidence had increased, for he added that his book "Will be rather good, I think." By September 7 his plans have become more secure—he tells Colles that he will finish it by the middle of November, and then two days later provides the first description of the plan and the nature of the book, ending his description with a statement that is interesting for its implications: "In short, I mean to make a readable little volume—one decidedly more alive (I trust) than that in the 'English Men of Letters Series.'" That volume was written by Adolphus William Ward, a Dickens scholar who had been one of Gissing's chief mentors at Owens College. Doubtless the man had been especially disappointed by the event of Gissing's scandalous termination, and there is some indication that he had been somewhat cold to his star pupil. Here was a chance, then, for Gissing to redeem himself in his old teacher's eyes by writing a book on Dickens that would be more lively, and in that sense better, than that of his master—while at the same time, since it was a critical study, it could not be regarded as competition. Doubtless this was one reason for Gissing's eagerness to get it done. He told Hick on September 10 that "*I* shall devote myself to solid work—for the first time for six years," since he had contracted to deliver the manuscript "by the end of November—a serious matter."

Gissing went to Italy to escape from the most profound and extended period of depression in his life, and he came there prepared to be happy. In September he had permanently separated himself from the terrors of the wife he thought was deranged. The burden of Edith and Alfred had already been taken in hand by Eliza Orme, and although he had to deal with this and other family matters by mail, he would now be at a considerable distance from all of that. As to his financial condition, we can only guess, but we recall that near the end of 1895 he had discovered he could make more than £500 a year, and in December he told his brother that he had put an end to all short story writing and was "taking the serious step of living upon capital for a year or so." He chose not to do that, and ten days later reported that he had £560 in his account. He then continued to write short stories, and, as noted above, *The Town Traveller* brought him a return of £350 for five weeks of work. Earlier in 1897, just after his removal to Budleigh Salterton, he had told Clara Collet: "It is a most fortunate thing that I am in no difficulties whatever with regard to money; & I don't think I shall be for some time to come." So it is tempting to speculate that by the end of 1897 he may have thought he could realize the small income from his Dickens book, a rewardingly serious work, and then enjoy his beloved Italy in peace—and, in view of his growing illness, perhaps even be rid of his insoluble problems, imagining his life coming to a close in something more like the luxury to which he was unaccustomed at home. As to the book, it is clear that during these few years Gissing was intent on writing in a variety of genres, and he was now working on one which he regarded as new territory—a book which might perhaps even satisfy his self-esteem by finally proving his success to the teachers he had disappointed by the Owens scandal. It was, in fact, a fitting cap to a period during which, while he expanded the range and volume of his writing to capitalize on his reputation—and did it under the terrifying stress of a raging wife and worries over his health, conditions which would have sunk a lesser man—he yet never lost sight of his serious work. His eye was still on excellence, and having planned in England the book that was to rescue Dickens from a low point of popularity and to establish his own reputation as a critic, it was appropriate that his first act in Italy was to write the book that justified the remaining months of his sojourn.

Gissing thus entered what is now regarded as one of the happiest periods of his life, and it seems providential that in Dunne, his earliest acquaintance in Italy, he found a man who was young, charming, Irish-American, Roman Catholic, and above all an aspiring writer—a formidable combination for an Englishman to encounter in those times. Surely here was a man whom he could impress with his reputation, and on whom he could exercise his wit, his playfulness, and even the "unwonted Anglo-mania" which Wells was surprised to find in him a few years later in Paris. Wells thought then that such a nostalgia had been stirred up by the sight of himself and his wife, but Gissing had lived and even suffered in America, and surely in Italy the Roman Catholic-Irish-American had something to do with his insistence on what Dunne later spoke of as Gissing's belief in the superiority of all things English. In fact, this historical clash between the English and American views of each other is responsible for much of the motivational tension throughout the memoirs, and for all its essential naiveté, it persisted well into this century. When Dunne finally wrote down his recollections, he not only remembered the old times but added a few extra barbs as well, referring once to the novel *Ruggles of Red Gap,* a classic spoof on the subject, demonstrating the superiority of all things American.

Even at the age of nineteen, however, Brian Bórú Dunne was hardly a young man without background, and he too had a personality to be reckoned with. His ancestors had come to America at a time when much of it could still be regarded as pioneer country, and several distinguished members of the family put their mark on it. Brian's grandfather, John O'Dunne, in 1829 emigrated from Ireland to Quebec, in Canada, where he intended to start a colony, but soon moved to New York, became a contractor in the building of the Erie Canal, engaged in a railway project that took him as far south as Harper's Ferry, went to California during the gold rush, and finally ended up with a vineyard and cattle ranch in California's Sonoma County. His son, Edmund, studied law in San Francisco, was elected to the legislature in 1862, and became a member of the constitutional convention for the new State of Nevada in 1864. In 1872 he married Josephine, daughter of Col. Francis Warner of Vicksburg, Mississippi, a girl who seems to have gone to France to work for a rich and influential family, the wedding taking place in Paris "with two French counts and a marquis as witnesses" (François, Cte de l'Isle du Fief, Marie Jean Baptiste Charles Emmanuel, Cte de la Serre, and Edmon [*sic*] Charles Marie, Mis de la Tourrette d'Ambert). Two years later he was appointed Chief Justice of the Arizona Territory by President Ulysses S. Grant. The Dunnes were zealous Catholic advocates, however, and Edmund was among the most fervent. His famous and flamboyant speech to the House of Representatives at Tucson advocating the use of public funds for Catholic schools so angered the legislators that he lost his judgeship, but at the same time so enhanced the esteem in which he was held by the Catholic Church that he was made Knight of the Order of St. Gregory in 1876, and a Commander in the Order two years later by Pope Leo XIII. He was also enabled to realize a long-standing ambition, doubtless inherited from his father, to found a Roman Catholic colony in this country. For his real estate work with Hamilton Disston, the millionaire head of a saw-making firm in Philadelphia, who had purchased four million acres of wilderness land in Florida, Dunne was granted fifty thousand acres, and in 1881 established the colony of San Antonio, as it is still called today. For that, Leo XIII created him a Papal Count, a hereditary title.

Judge Dunne was an exceptionally well educated man who brought to the Florida wilderness an extraordinary personal library and was instrumental in the founding of St. Leo College there in 1889. At about that time, Dunne's connection with the colony came to an end, but by special arrangement he was able to send his two sons, Eugene (age 13) and Brian (age 10), to St. Mary's College in Belmont, North Carolina, where they took a full classical course of studies together with such "other secular instruction" as they might need. Eugene went on to become a distinguished lawyer and judge in Baltimore and eventually a member of the Maryland Supreme Court. Brian graduated in 1893, but we know little of his activities during the next few years. He may well have worked for a newspaper in Baltimore at some time, for as a boy of ten he had run a newspaper in the colony of San Antonio. We do know that in 1895 his father sent him to study at a school in Bruges, Belgium. According to his own account he spent a year in Germany learning German dialects, and considerable time in France as well. Two years after his arrival in Europe, having studied and traveled extensively there, he presented himself to Gissing in 1897 as an aspiring journalist. He stayed in Rome several months after Gissing left, and when he was called home from Italy near the end of 1898, presumably in preparation for his eventual work in his father's projected new colony in Alabama, we know he wrote for the *Baltimore Sun,* and then for the *Times* and other newspapers in Washington, D.C.

But soon Brian's destiny was linked once again with his father's. Judge Dunne, on leaving San Antonio in 1889, first attended a huge reunion of the family, whose members came from around the country to Mackinac Island, at that time a resort open chiefly to the rich, and then returned to practicing law, first in Ottawa, Canada, then for a while in Toledo, Ohio, where he argued a celebrated public school case before the Ohio Supreme Court, and by 1893 set up an office in Jacksonville, Florida. It was shortly thereafter, in 1895, that he sent Brian on his three-year journey to familiarize himself with Europe and its languages. Judge Dunne left Jacksonville for Baltimore in 1899, but some time around the turn of the century he was engaged in forming another Catholic colony near Castleberry, Alabama. The settlement at San Antonio had been made up chiefly of Irish, French, and German settlers, and Judge Dunne's knowledge of several European languages aided him in this work. He had lived in Rome and Paris and spoke Spanish, French, and Italian perfectly, but was somewhat weak in German. Nonetheless, the industriousness of German immigrants had impressed him, and this new colony in Alabama, to which he gave the name of Hochheim, seems to have been designed exclusively as a German settlement, with the motto *"Viehzucht, Korn, Obst u Weinbau"*— "Cattle-raising, Grain, Fruit, and Wine growing." As for Brian, whatever the condition of his journalistic career might have been, he seems to have given it up at this time, for we know he was deeply involved in helping his father with this new enterprise. In the heading of the only surviving letter he wrote to Gissing, dated January 1, 1902, "B. O'Dunne" is listed as Secretary and Treasurer of the colony.

When Judge Dunne sent Brian to a school in Belgium and on to the long tour of Europe, it seems that his intention was to educate his son not only in the cultures and the languages of the Old World, but particularly in the various dialects of Germany, the chief source of immigrants to populate this new colony of Hochheim. The school Brian attended in Bruges was known as the *Collège des Princes* because it was attended by princes of the de Croÿ family, one of the most aristocratic in Europe, with branches in nearly every country (the then reigning Duke de Croÿ was German); doubtless the Judge chose the school because Elizabeth Parnall de Croÿ, an Anglo-Irish woman, was an ardent admirer of Brian's aunt, Sister Amadeus, a famous Ursuline nun whom she visited in Montana in 1904. Some of the Belgian princes in this family later had an interest in America, one teaching in a music school and another acquiring mining interests near Denver, where he became a Society favorite. We know that a strong relationship developed between some members of the family and the Dunnes, for Princess Marie, Elisabeth's daughter, who was cited for heroic conduct during World War I, was later the godmother of Brian's daughter, Katherine Dunne.

At any rate, even if Brian was not sent to Belgium primarily to study among his father's acquaintances in the Croÿ family, he certainly met them there, spent a vacation with two Belgian princes of the family in one of their *châteaux* in the north of France, and later found another of them, also of the Belgian branch, to be of service to him in Rome. We know nothing of his activities in Germany, but in Rome, trying to get a rare ticket to a Papal Mass, he claimed to have the support of "a friend of the Kaiser's," which clearly meant that he had known some of the German branch of the Croÿ family. And these are the credentials he carried with him when he met Gissing in Siena in the autumn of 1897. No doubt he was, as he says in his memoir of Gissing, very young and even naive, but he was at least beginning to be a man of the world, he was very bright, he had been educated in classical languages, he had studied in Europe, he was the son of a charismatic father whose bearing and authority have been described as majestic, and he was not about to be wholly intimidated even by a famous English writer in Italy—although he was sufficiently wise and inexperienced to be somewhat awed by him, and he was duly impressed by H. G. Wells and perhaps even by Arthur Conan Doyle, who were among Gissing's companions for a month there.

Dunne's first encounter with Gissing took place on September 29, 1897, an event remarkable in no way except that it occurred just a few days after Gissing established himself in the boarding-house on the Via delle Belle Arti. Gissing had arrived in Siena on September 25, found his room the next day, moved into it on the twenty-seventh, began work on his *Dickens* the next day, and on the twenty-ninth made this simple entry into his diary: "A new boarder —young American." It was, of course, inevitable that they should meet and talk together, at least during meals, and within two days Gissing had learned that "The young American here is called Brian O'Dunne [the old family name Dunne used in Italy]. He has been rambling in Europe for two years. Belongs to Florida. Plays the zither." Yet we hear nothing more of him for another twelve days, and then only in a diary entry devoted to one Vincenzo Tateo, an old Garibaldino from Naples whom Dunne had seen "when calling on American friends of his there." Indeed, the most curious aspect of this friendship which developed over several months in Siena and Rome is that we know so little of it from Gissing himself. In the letters from this period there is nothing at all about Dunne. Later, after the Roman months, Gissing wrote a brief note to Mrs. Wells on July 22, 1898, saying thanks "for O'D's letters etc," and then two letters to Wells which do reflect a friendship in which Dunne had elicited Gissing's esteem. On November 6, after just a word about W. M. Evans's decision to enter the field of journalism, he was reminded to pay Dunne a handsome compliment: "Then, I have a copy of the Baltimore *Sun,* containing a descriptive article by Brian O'Dunne—rather good. He, the excellent Brian, will un-doubtedly make a journalist." And finally, on December 9, a more extended comment illustrating Gissing's typical spirit of generosity to fellow writers: "I have heard once or twice from O'Dunne. He has made a beginning of journalism at Baltimore, and writes with all the glee of a youth in such case. He finds your books abundantly read in Baltimore, and, I can see, chuckles over his ability to declare acquaintance with the author. From the samples of his journalism which he has sent (sketches of his life in Europe) I have no doubt he will do well enough."

In the diary entries, however, we get a little clearer idea of their relationship, and although the record is sketchy enough, it provides at least a slight background for reading Dunne's memoir of his friend. Sometimes Gissing's entries add details about the people mentioned by Dunne, as in the case of Cappelli, the medical student who joked about some Italian brigands having copies of Dante in their pockets. On the day when this fellow boarder finished his military service, Gissing and Dunne bought him a bottle of Marsala, and at dinner the next day heard the sad news of the landlord's death. After dinner Gissing sat with Dunne in his room. Unable to work the next day, he walked with Dunne to Porta Fontebranda and then attended the funeral, where Cappelli suggested that they "put our names among those subscribing for a wreath." Two days later, on October 20, Gissing describes in detail *la caccia*, the event Dunne mentions in the memoir, and the following day Dunne left Siena for Rome. He had stayed at the boardinghouse for three weeks.

During the next two weeks Gissing heard from Dunne a few times ("writes like a very decent fellow") and when he was about to finish his *Dickens* wrote him to say that he would be in Rome on November 8. Dunne was waiting for him there, and after a day of sightseeing with him, Gissing left for Naples on the tenth. Except for the letter he received on December 9, that is the last we hear of Dunne until Gissing returned to Rome, where after a night at the Hotel Minerva the two of them spent the day of the sixteenth finding a room for Gissing. Two weeks later Dunne offered him a ticket for "the Pope's Mass" (to celebrate the fiftieth anniversary of Leo XIII's first mass), but on January 1 he was too ill to go. On January

12 Gissing describes his evening with Dunne at the Orpheo Theatre, another event which Dunne dwells on in the memoir, and then four days later at the wretched variety concert in the Via Due Macelli. The only other event described in the diary was the "Requiem Mass, for Pio Nono" on February 7, once again with a ticket given him by Dunne, who describes at length in the memoir his difficulty in getting tickets to these Papal masses. When Gissing received four copies of his *Dickens* on February 22, he gave one to Dunne, and that is the last we hear of Dunne until after Gissing returned home in early April. Curiously, there is no mention of him during the visit to Rome of H. G. Wells in March, although Dunne was certainly active among the company there, apparently on occasion acting as a guide for the Wellses—indeed, Wells remembered him years later, and Dunne in turn sought Wells's support for his books. During the remaining months of 1898 Gissing records receipt of three letters from Dunne, the last containing a copy of the *Baltimore Sun* with a review of *The Town Traveller,* and then his name disappears from the diary altogether.

From the distance of a hundred years, it may seem curious, and even inexplicable, that Gissing's diary does not record the kind of friendship and companionship on which Dunne drew thirty-five years later in his detailed and often dramatic recollections of the English novelist who was then at the height of his fame. But doubtless the fact of Gissing's fame is itself a satisfactory key to this apparent problem. In Siena, where the simple life was not complicated by social obligations or by famous people or by visiting friends of friends at home or even by adventures in places famous in history, no other such companion is named in Gissing's diary. But it is clear that Gissing talked with Dunne, walked with him, saw the sights of Siena and the surrounding places of interest with him, and shared stories and recollections—and Dunne reciprocated Gissing's hospitality by inviting the famous man to visit him in his own room. Gissing must have spoken with Dunne daily, but the quotidian events of such a comradeship with an unknown young man are hardly likely to figure largely in the personal concerns of a diary. Even when he came across matters of some historical interest, it was the event itself which figured in the diary, not the presence of a daily companion, especially one who had not yet even begun to acquire his destined stature in the world. Gissing provides an interesting example of this when he describes his walk with Dunne just before attending the funeral of their landlord: "Unable to work, so walked with O'Dunne from Porta Ovile to Porta Fontebranda; then into the Public Library, where saw the splendid old MSS, a letter of S. Catherine etc.—At 5 o'clock took place the funeral—24 hrs after death." Here the presence of Dunne is merely a narrative fact.

Dunne, then, at the age of twenty (he turned twenty in Rome) did not claim a memorable space in Gissing's diary. We cannot know exactly how Gissing fared in Dunne's diary, but Siena was hardly the town to provide even a distinguished writer many opportunities to reveal his public acclaim, and there Dunne knew him chiefly as a scholarly companion. In Rome it might well have been otherwise, but the diary he kept has been lost, and it is to be regretted that Dunne did not leave us a great pile of spontaneous notes and sketches of his friend. But a young man of unproven qualities, bright, enthralled by immediate experiences, and sure of his memory, was hardly likely to think of himself as a future memorialist. Yet his extraordinary life brought him later into association with a great number of famous and remarkable people, and when in the fullness of his own time he set about recording his memories of them, it is fortunate that he could present us with a Gissing in the vivid details of real life. Gissing remembered him when he met Gabrielle Fleury and asked him to consult his brother Eugene, by then a Baltimore lawyer, about the divorce laws in America. Dunne remembered Gissing when he wrote a letter in 1902 recalling the experiences in Rome and summarizing his life to that point. It is there we learn that in Italy he did at least keep a diary recording his days with Gissing, which unfortunately does not survive. Nonetheless, it was clearly with him when he wrote the memoir.

Even apart from the diary, however, Dunne's remarkable memory retained its sharpness, as we are told by his son, until the day he died. During the rest of his long career he had many occasions to remember those Italian days with Gissing, and a brief summary of that career will help to define the man who, as a seasoned writer and "collector of people," came to write the memoirs some time in the 1930s. When Dunne was recalled from his long tour of Europe, noted above, he began his career as a journalist with the *Baltimore Sun* and with the *Times* and other newspapers in Washington, D.C. It was, Gissing himself suggested, a considerable career. To understand Dunne's future in journalism, we need to remember that there, in Washington, D.C., he earned himself a reputation as one of the most successful interviewers in town. It was for the *Times,* for example, that he conducted his remarkable Thanksgiving "interview" with Mark Twain, which became known in journalistic circles as the interview that Twain had written for him (see Appendix 4).

Nonetheless, Dunne's journalistic career at this point was a short one. According to his own account in the letter of January 23, 1902, the newspaper work proved to be uncongenial, "turning night into day," as he wrote, and the "terrific mental strain" coupled with the intense heat of Baltimore brought on a spell of illness diagnosed as "nervous prostration, dyspepsia from irregular meals & a general break down." That was in June of 1901. His father, after a decade of employment as a lawyer in several cities in Canada and the United States, had joined his two sons in Baltimore in 1899, but it is clear that at the age of sixty-four he was on his way to realizing the long-standing ambition of establishing another colony, twenty years after founding the colony of San Antonio in Florida. In 1901 Brian was deeply involved as treasurer of the German colony which he christened Hochheim, exchanging the heat of Baltimore for the heat of Alabama. It was, however, a brief and ill-fated venture. Judge Dunne suffered a paralyzing stroke in May of 1903, at which time Eugene O'Dunne prophesied that his father would never leave the hospital, writing to his brother Brian in August from St. Agnes' Sanitarium: "I think very often of our rough venture in Alabama. What an experience! How well we know that place now, and *the people!* Do you ever want to see them again!" From his hospital bed in December Judge Dunne wrote his last letter to Brian: "I have had a new feeling toward you since our adventure in Alabama—that of a comrade in a great, long adventurous and try- ing experience. . . . Don't misunderstand about life. It is not all hard lines by any means. . . . You are in a country of heroes. Re- member that you too are of a long line of chiefs and that you must *never say die!*" Judge Edmund O'Dunne died on October 4, 1904, at the age of sixty-nine.

By this time Brian Dunne's siblings had established themselves in their permanent occupations for life. His brother, who inherited their father's Papal title, retained the family's historic name, and called himself Eugene Viscount O'Dunne, had an extraordinarily successful law practice in Baltimore and later, as we said, became a member of the Maryland Supreme Court. (On May 22, 1945, H. L. Mencken wrote to Brian: "Your brother is retiring in June, and the assembled lawyers, police captains, bootleggers and clergy of Baltimore are preparing to give him a dinner.") His two sisters had become Ursuline nuns, Mother Amata living in the Heart of Jesus convent in Toledo, and Mother Amadeus, founder of the Ursuline Missions in Montana and Alaska, becoming the subject of two books. But Brian himself must have felt cast adrift by the demise of the new German colony in Alabama. In spite of the optimistic esti- mate of his health in the letter to Gissing in 1902, where he said he had gained fifty pounds in Hochheim, he was still suffering the effects of the dyspepsia he had contracted as a newsman in Balti- more in 1901. We surmise that it was in about 1903 or 1904, some time after the death of his father, that he returned to newspaper work in Washington, D.C., and that in late 1905 or early 1906 he embarked on the travel segment of what he later called his journey in search of health, ending only when he took up permanent resi- dence in Santa Fe in 1909.

Many events of that remarkable and eventful journey can be found in Brian Dunne's first book, *Cured! The 70 Adventures of a Dys- peptic,* published in 1914, a book which he told Wells was "my life's story from the year 1901 to 1911." Perhaps unfortunately, that book was never meant to be taken as a literal autobiography, but took the shape of a series of hilarious adventures satirizing and exposing the often bumbling fraudulence in American medicine at that time, written in the heightened and exaggerated tone of American humor popular then, and having the effect of a comic indictment of the medical profession. Many of the situations are indeed comical, but the humor in presentation is all Dunne's, and beneath it lies the eight-year record of a resourceful, imaginative, and courageous young man, surviving as a journalist in many cities from coast to coast, and proving his talents in some of the most enterprising new professions in the country. The book was dedicated to "The Physicians of the Johns Hopkins Hospital, Who Saved Me from the Surgeon's Knife." H. G. Wells wrote a brief foreword in which, astonishingly, he denied ever having met Dunne, but praised the book as "shining with cheerfulness and telling of years of unbroken ill health," calling it "a real contribution to the difficult art of living." In a personal letter, Van Wyck Brooks said it was "in the best tradition of the classical American humorists" and that "In this line Mark Twain never did anything better." In 1947 Dunne sent a copy of the second edition to George Bernard Shaw, who replied: "Thank you for the book. I wrote a British counterpart to it myself years ago, called Doctors' Delusions. . . . My complaint (headaches once a month or so) was only an excuse for sampling the treatments. They ceased when I was 70. All the practitioners I had consulted at once claimed to have cured me."

It is not necessary to summarize the whole of Brian's book in order to suggest the incredible variety of his experiences, but one difficulty in dealing with it as a record of his activities is that the temporal organization and the tone are determined by the central point of his satire, and so it is only the medical issues which drive it on. Unfortunately for us, he did not stress the various kinds of work in which he was engaged while he roamed the country in search of a cure, but those and other events in his life are often referred to somewhat obliquely, whenever the latent humor in them could justify their inclusion. In view of the broad style of American humor, however, which depends heavily on comic exaggeration, it is necessary to remind the reader again that, underlying the humor, is the real record of Dunne's actual personal experiences, and with due care we are therefore entitled to view the book as providing a glimpse into Dunne's life between Hochheim and Santa Fe. Some of the events, along with Dunne's earlier experiences, are mentioned in the radio address by Alfred Morang, the Santa Fe artist, printed at the end of this book, and there too the bewildering range of Dunne's activities may lead one to suspect that Morang himself, perhaps aided by Dunne's narrative, exaggerated in the interest of presenting a suitable encomium. But there also it can be ascertained that Brian actually did whatever he said he did. He was a journalist who reported accurately on himself; events in Dunne's book are corroborated by newspaper clippings and other documents among the surviving papers. In Baltimore, before the Hochheim debacle, Dunne acted as an informal secretary or friend to Cardinal Gibbons, editing his Sunday sermons for publication and spending many an evening discussing, among other things, Vatican politics. They also took up questions of health and longevity (Gibbons was in frail health, but lived to the age of eighty-seven), and we print in an appendix to this volume an article by Dunne showing that the Cardinal was well advanced in his dietary views, giving the kind of advice we hear around us today. We have also a letter of recommendation in the Cardinal's hand, saying "Mr. Brian Dunne has been known to me for some years, & I regard him as a young man of ripe intelligence, of extraordinary diligence & laudable ambition, & well qualified for newspaper work." Later, Dunne acted in a similar capacity with G. B. Pitaval, the Archbishop of Santa Fe, who recommended him as "my friend Mr. Brian Ború Dunne, a journalist and author, who has been spending some time in Santa Fe, where he is well and favorably known. . . . I regard him and esteem him highly." In *Cured!*, when Dunne speaks of the advice he got from "a certain archbishop," we may be sure it was Pitaval he had in mind.

Early in his book, Brian says that he had worked for months on the *Baltimore Sun,* and then describes the same discomfort he had mentioned in the letter to Gissing of 1902: "Finally the late hours, the irregular and hurried meals, the worry over scoops and the hurry-hurry of the metropolitan newspaperman's life began to tell on me." An alarming attack of illness led him to enter an infirmary, and after failed attempts at treatment, he says, "It was decided that I resign from the paper and spend a year on a plantation in Balmy Alabama." He does not name Hochheim, but as he says he was only twenty-three at the time, and as he was born on July 13, 1878, this account confirms the date of his involvement in the colony as 1901, or the early months of 1902. There his illness was diagnosed as "acid dyspepsia." He omits any description of his duties there, of course, as irrelevant to the satiric point of the book, and after a very long comic narrative of inept and incompetent medical treatment, he describes his departure: "And so it came to pass that toward the end of July I was traveling to Denver, seeking a new doctor, a new clime and a new cure."

Nothing is given a date in Dunne's book, and there is no distinct time sequence to the events, but we have speculated above that his departure from Alabama must have followed shortly after the illness and death of his father. Our purpose here, however, is not to trace his actions in detail but only to suggest the scope of his experiences, to point out some which are corroborated by his writings and by other documents, and to suggest some elements of his stylistic technique which we see in the Gissing memoirs. In his travels after Denver he mentions Spokane, Washington, his work on a dairy farm in Utah, a trip into Canada, his wretched attempt to earn his living as a cowboy in Helena, Montana, then a journey east to Minneapolis, finally ending up back in Baltimore and Washington, D.C. In Washington he read Annie Payson Call's book *Power through Repose,* which was useful to him when he wrote his interview with William Jennings Bryan, printed here as an appendix. At that time he also made a "call on a cardinal," from whom he received the same advice he records in his article on Cardinal Gibbons and diet: eschew red meat, avoid heavy meals late at night, take daily walks, and see no doctors. In Washington, D.C., he renewed his acquaintance with former colleagues in the newspaper business and was reminded of his famous interview which "made a sensation, for it was all the work of that peerless newspaperman and author, Mark Twain, who had granted the interview on condition that he himself be allowed to write it."

Once again troubled by "that awful summer heat," however, he "wrote to different firms seeking a position as traveling salesman and finally landed a job which was to take me from Boston to New Orleans and as far west as Ohio." For this job he went immediately to Pennsylvania, doubtless to Scranton, which is still the headquarters of the International Correspondence School, a company with which Dunne seems to have stayed for a considerable time, specializing particularly in the teaching of foreign languages by means of the phonograph. We have a letter dated October 18, 1906, from Droop and Sons, a large music establishment in New York City, introducing him to the *Chargé d'Affaires* at the Mexican Embassy "for the purpose of demonstrating the Edison 'language course.'" There is also a cordial letter from the Eastern Talking Machine Co. in Boston, dated November 6, thanking him "for the work done in demonstrating the I. C. S. Foreign Language Study Outfits," hoping the company will be "fortunate enough" to receive further demonstrations, "and that the Home Office will see fit to furnish your good self as the demonstrator." In September of 1906 Dunne demonstrated the ICS French course on wax cylinders to Wilbur and Orville Wright in their office above the bicycle shop in Dayton, Ohio. According to Elsbeth Freudenthal, the Wright brothers' biographer (*Flight into History*, 1949), who interviewed him in Santa Fe, Dunne found the brothers, dressed like business executives, sitting behind a long oak desk on which were stacks of drawings and blueprints. According to Brian B. Dunne II, he asked whether the airplane could be used in war to drop grenades on the enemy, but was told that "carrying such weight would not be possible—the airplane could only be used for reconnaissance." The brothers politely declined to give him a photograph of the plane to show to Alexander Graham Bell, but they assured him that "The future will be magnificent."

Near the end of his book Brian remarks: "I still stuck to newspaper work." Judging from the evidence we have, that appears to have been his chief occupation in cities wherever he traveled. He spent a considerable time in Ithaca, New York, where he was employed in several capacities: "I had a newspaper friend who was editing an afternoon paper in a 'college town' in northern New York. . . . My newspaper friend gladly gave me a position as interviewer on his paper, and also assigned me the post of music critic. There were two conservatories in the town and many musical affairs at the 'varsity." Although he adds that "In Washington, Jim Morley had made me do some 'musical criticism,'" it was in Ithaca that he acquired the musical education he found useful in his article on William Jennings Bryan. Doubtless he carried with him letters of recommendation, and clearly he acquired others along the way. The following letter, for example, dated May 14, 1906, and written on the letterhead of the Tribune Publishing Co. of Bainbridge, Georgia, not only establishes that his travels took him into the South, but also suggests the kinds of positions that were open to him:

> Brian Dunne, the city editor of the Tribune, has been an acquaintance of mine for some months and I regard him as a man possessed of a wide and useful knowledge. His ability as a linguist is unquestioned. Some time ago this was well demonstrated when a party who called themselves "Chaldeans" landed here and could not make themselves understood until Mr. Dunne was secured as their interpreter—the medium being French.
>
> He is an able teacher of modern languages, as I have had opportunity to ascertain. I myself have taken lessons from him in colloquial French.
>
> His conduct here has been exemplary and he enjoys the friendship of the best and most influential citizens of this city, county and state.

Dunne seems also to have solicited this kind of backing from such friends as he thought important enough to be of help. We have seen above that Gissing noticed his tendency to "chuckle over his ability to declare acquaintance" with H. G. Wells, and the following letter of August 23, 1907, seems to us to be the kind of "recommendation" that Wells would choose to offer:

> I remember very vividly meeting you in Rome with George Gissing way back in '97, and how impressed he was by your assiduous study of Italian ways and customs, music and language. I should think your work and experiences in those days would do much to fit you for the position you now seek.

The following letter by Frank R. Morse, addressed "To Whom It May Concern," may perhaps serve as an indication of what was expressed in the more formal recommendations, although it is undated and was clearly written at a somewhat later date:

> While I was Sunday Editor of the Washington [D.C.] Times, BrianBorú Dunne was rated as the most successful interviewer in the Nation's Capital. He was the only Washington newspaper man who succeeded in extracting an interview (self-written) from Mark Twain, when the author of "Life on the Mississippi" journeyed for the last time to the banks of the Potomac. He was the only Washington newspaper man who succeeded in getting an interview out of El Hadji Abdul Pasha, nephew of Menelik II, Emperor of Ethiopia, whose credentials written in Arabic baffled, for a time, even the State Department officials of the "Teddy" Roosevelt administration. BrianBorú Dunne . . . traveled all over the United States, writing for large and small papers, and later headed the newspaper bureau for the first San Diego Exposition, sending weekly broadcasts to six hundred papers.

Dunne had met Roosevelt on three occasions in Washington, D.C., but was particularly proud that, after a picture-taking ceremony at the Exposition, Roosevelt had asked him to walk on the "grand pathway" around the Rose Garden to discuss Dunne's views on the candidacy and the prospects of Hiram Johnson, who was running for governor of California.

When Brian Dunne chose to settle down in Santa Fe, he took full advantage of the opportunities to employ all the skills he had developed in his father's colonies, his European tour, and his many years as a journalist and peripatetic entrepreneur, becoming in a few years one of the town's leading citizens, a role he filled until the end of his life. We may suggest enough of his life there to characterize the man who, thirty-five years after the event, was finally to write a memoir of Gissing—and, indeed, memoirs of other famous men he had known in his role as the prominent figure in the "City Different," which finally developed an international reputation for its healthful climate and, because of its artistic and literary community and the nearby Indian cultures, host to many world celebrities. He would, of course, immediately set up with Archbishop Pitaval the kind of relationship he had had with Cardinal Gibbons (an obituary said he was "a special secretary to Archbishop J. B. Pitaval from 1909–1912"). But he also became city editor of the *Santa Fe New Mexican,* the oldest newspaper in the Southwest, and he quickly formed a friendship with the powerful Senator Bronson Cutting, who had come to Santa Fe in 1910 for his health and, like Dunne, stayed there for the rest of his life. For a time Cutting's illness from tuberculosis kept him indoors, where his sister Justine, Dunne, and H. H. Dorman, a realtor, entertained him and brought others to see him. When Dunne discovered that Cutting was a devoted reader of Gissing, he regaled him with stories from the Italian days. At one time Dunne and the ex-governor, Miguel Antonio Otero, shared bachelor quarters with Cutting, and were thus part of Cutting's expanding social life. In 1912 Cutting bought the New Mexican Printing Company, thus making Dunne technically an employee. But by the fall of 1919 Dunne had become exhausted as a journalist, saying he had "worn out fourteen horses in 10 years chasing around the 55 places to be visited daily," and suddenly left for Tahiti, where he said he had business interests, in January of 1920. He carried with him a letter to the governor of Tahiti from Benjamin F. Paukey, the acting governor of New Mexico: "Mr. Dunne enjoys an enviable reputation wherever he is known, and I cannot speak too highly of his character as a man and as a citizen." Whatever those "business interests" were, however, Dunne was soon disillusioned, and before the half year was out he eagerly returned to his old quarters and to the city editorship of the *New Mexican,* and especially to his friendship with Senator Cutting, managing the complex personal affairs when the senator was out of town.

From the beginning of Dunne's residence in Santa Fe, he was vitally interested in working for the statehood of New Mexico, as his father had done in Nevada, and he died on the last day of New Mexico's golden anniversary as a state. For many years, and until his death, he spent part of every day in the lobby of La Fonda, one of the great old Pueblo-styled hotels (which he called his "club"), holding forth to all who stopped by for a chat, and his famous "conversations" there attracted a large following. He was called "a leading citizen and a landmark of Santa Fe," and "numerous youngsters had perfected imitations of Bee Bee's walk and distinctive dress." But although he was known as "the reporter-politician-master conversationalist and town greeter," it is important to remember that he was first and foremost a journalist, and particularly a noted interviewer. Besides being the city editor for the *Santa Fe New Mexican* for many years, he wrote a daily column in it from 1940 to 1952, when he switched to a weekly column.

Perhaps his chief personal characteristic, however, was his interest in everyone he met, especially those who were eccentric or exotic or simply different, and all his roles in Santa Fe enabled him to earn the title which Alfred Morang gave him, a "collector of people." And in those days many of the famous ones came to Santa Fe, where Dunne met them, talked with them, often befriended them, and finally intended to write about them. An article in the *New Mexican* in 1964 noted that he had "filled 72 notebooks with observations of the people he had interviewed in Santa Fe and before his arrival," and listed the names of William Jennings Bryan, the Wright brothers, Marconi (who told him in an interview "The television will be important, but the radio will *always* be more important!"), Mark Twain, John D. Rockefeller, Paderewski, the grandson of the Kaiser, Teddy Roosevelt, and many others. A newspaper report in 1938 noted that Dunne was going to write a book on New Mexico's "Old Timers," such as "Charley Siringo, Captain Fred Fornoff, F. Coomer, John Willis (famous hunter and friend of Theodore Roosevelt), and half a dozen territorial and state governors, mining magnates, and many writers." Indeed, Dunne spent a good many of his later years writing memoirs. By 1952 he wrote to Mrs. Frank Blair, the wife of the Chicago stockbroker turned treasure hunter, that "I wish to include Mr. Blair among the interesting people I have met in a book I am now writing about *people*. The forewords are by Sinclair Lewis, H. G. Wells and A. R. Orage and others." The book was to be entitled "They All Came to Santa Fe," and the final manuscript contained two thousand entries, often reading like those of a latter-day Samuel Pepys keeping a town diary. It is a unique view of the extremely diverse figures who sought some ineffable quality in Santa Fe. Dunne continually benefited by the strange attraction Santa Fe had for artists, musicians, writers, financiers, and politicians. He could just sit in his chair at the La Fonda. They came to him.

This book was never published, but fortunately for us one of the many personalities of whom he drafted recollections was George Gissing. When Dunne returned from Rome, perhaps he wrote nothing at all on Gissing because he thought the author's reputation in America was too slender to warrant it. We do not even know whether he wrote the review of *The Town Traveller* in the *Baltimore Sun* of 1898, and in his surviving papers there are no notes and few records of any kind from that period. It was, of course, too early for anything like a memoir, but one might think that the occasion of Gissing's death would have given him the opportunity to use his diary in a journalistic way. In 1903, however, he had moved to Hochheim, and even if he thought of some kind of memorial, he was without a significant outlet. The earliest evidence that he wrote down anything at all about Gissing is in the letter mentioned above, which he mailed him from Hochheim on January 23, 1902, in which he mentions his diary. His quotation from it captures some of the playfulness and the wit he associated with Gissing:

> How often I think of you & our "Roman Roaming." I read in my diary only the other day "Gissing is complaining of a cold—says his life is coming to an end" and "Gissing & I saw the King to-day. Gissing says his eyes are red because he, the King, drinks heavily & maybe goes under the table!" Then there is an item or two about old Bullion [Bullen, Gissing's publisher], "The" champion eater at that Cafe where one of the Muses poured out the wine for all of us, but more so for Buller or Bullion as he always took ½ glasses to gain wine! Then there are a few interesting remarks about the subject discussed that night by the Cavalieri Erranti: "To wash one's neck, or not,—that's the question!" Do you remember that old boy, Rinaldi, my landlord, who responded when I asked *dov'è il cesso? = Non c'è!* [Where is the toilet? = There isn't one!] O, it makes me laugh to think of those times, which would not have been much if it were not for your company, philosophical as well as "instructively amusing." You must let me know what you found out about that queer genius, the lady from Montenegro who used to make you speechless with amazement! Lambart was the name, I believe.

Dunne also kept up a very slender correspondence with H. G. Wells, and from this we get our only evidence of continued interest in Gissing, leading up to his later decision to write the memoir. On June 15, 1912, when he sent to Wells a manuscript of *Cured!* and asked for "a written word of approval thereof without having to 'lie like hell' (as Gissing said he used to have to do with MSS & books sometimes submitted to him)," he begins his letter with another remembered detail about Gissing: "Do you remember George Gissing's friend who made you walk up five flights of stairs in Via Gregoriano in Rome in 1898; who played (?) the Zither for your benefit, with Gissing remarking 'You're out of practice my boy'?" These are mere tidbits, however, and serve only to show that Dunne on occasion held on to the memory of those Italian days with Gissing, a memory preserved in his diary and doubtless refreshed by his habit of narrating the episodes to Senator Cutting, one of Gissing's strongest devotees in America. It was not until twenty-one years later that we hear about Gissing again, but this time with the first suggestion that Dunne was actually interested in writing about him. This was in the letter to Wells of January 21, 1933, containing the remarkable sentence quoted above. That sentence should now be seen in the context of the whole paragraph from which it was quoted:

> At the suggestion of Orage, I am writing a book "Personal Recollections of George Gissing." I shall send you the MSS as I know you will be amused. I look upon Gissing as one of the most cheerful, luxury-loving, witty people I ever met. But he may have led a hell of a life. I read his *Letters.* Pretty dull stuff!

It is uncertain whether there is some causal connection between Dunne's reading of the Gissing family letters (1927) and his sudden decision to write down his own Recollections. A. R. Orage had been the editor of the *New Age;* he was a Fabian, and a man highly respected in artistic, political, and intellectual affairs, when in 1922 he went off to spend a year at Fontainebleau under the spell of Gurdjieff, a charismatic psychological/religious cultist, and then came to New York to spread the teachings. He lectured and taught in America for many years from 1924, chiefly in New York, but with trips also to Boston and Chicago, and later to other parts of the country. Gradually working out from under the Gurdjieff spell, he began rereading the somewhat subversive economic theory of Social Credit by Clifford Hugh Douglas, held classes and lectured on the Douglas principles of credit and finance, taught successfully at a private school of journalism, and returned to England in 1930. Shortly after that, he revisited America for several months to give a course of lectures on English literature, and went back to England in 1931 to found the *New English Weekly.* Dunne, in his long memoir of Senator Cutting, records Orage's visit to Santa Fe, calling him a "brilliant London editor" and commenting on "the train of deep thought such men as Orage aroused." Cutting said that Orage "edited about the best of the stuff in the magazine line that came over from England." When Dunne interviewed him, Orage vented his "ideas about 'shutting up' neurotic women," and said that "women who go into convents, and sacrifice themselves in the cause of Christ, were pure lunatics." In Dunne's letter of 1933, where he says his "Personal Recollections" were to be written "At the suggestion of Orage," he notes also that "Mencken and Orage have given lines for the jacket" of his new book, *Popes, Pugilists and Presidents*.

That book too seems never to have been published, nor did anything come of his "Personal Recollections" of Gissing. But then in 1934 Wells published his *Experiment in Autobiography*, and the long section on Gissing seems to have stirred Dunne into action. On April 8, 1935, he sent the following telegram to Wells at Spade House, Sandgate:

YOUR AUTOBIOGRAPHICAL CHAPTER GEORGE GISSING
SUPERB WISH TO DO SOME AUTOBIOGRAPHICAL NOTES OF
MY OWN FOR LONDON TIMES KINDLY BOOST THIS IDEA
CABLE REPLY BEST WISHES.

Curiously, he sent a second, follow-up telegram to Wells later the same day:

POSTSCRIPT ORAGE ASKED THAT THESE RECOLLECTIONS
BE WRITTEN SHOWING GISSINGS REACTION BRITISH
ROYALTY AND CAPITALISTIC SYSTEM REGARDS.

Since Orage had died on November 6, 1934, it is clear that he had made his request in 1933, when he first suggested the article, and Dunne may have written some kind of article on Gissing at either time. Perhaps the two articles printed here may be taken as evidence that he did so, but in any case he seems to have decided that he could not, or would not, tailor his recollections of Gissing to support any economic or political ideology unsuitable to his own experience as an American—and if he submitted anything else to

Orage, it might well have been rejected as unsuitable for the *New English Weekly*. It is still unclear why he mentioned Orage's wishes in a second telegram to Wells, unless he was asking advice or approval, or merely conveying his intention. In mentioning that he was writing for the *Times,* he must have meant the *Literary Supplement,* and perhaps he had in mind a literary letter occasioned by Wells's book.

That is the record as we know it. Twice in his middle years Dunne contemplated some kind of memoir of his friend, but for unknown reasons published nothing, although H. G. Wells's autobiography appeared to give him some occasion for it. By 1959, as we said above, Royal Gettmann knew about the existence of a written memoir, but although he read it, he made nothing of it, perhaps because Dunne was still planning to use it in a book of the famous men he had known. And so things remained until 1994, when his son, Brian B. Dunne II, began looking through the many leather trunks of his father's papers, in response to a request by the editors of the Gissing letters. What he found there is what we print here, consisting mainly of the draft memoir itself and a few other versions of it, chiefly in the form of articles.

We have described these in the headnotes attached to each item, but as there are no dates given for any of them, we cannot present them in any certain order of composition. We judge that the memoir itself is the earliest one, not only because it is longer and more complete, but also because Dunne mentions it in the earlier of the two letters to Wells. The situation is complicated by the long list, in seven typed pages, of the topics which Dunne apparently meant to include. Because the memoir does not deal with all of these, we conclude that the list names all the recollections he could muster, while the memoir deals only with the significant ones he would work into a coherent piece in the act of composition. That memoir, MS-A, is in two parts, one for the Siena days, the other for Rome. It seems to have been constructed as a first draft, however, and so we follow it with a second manuscript, MS-B, which we take to be a more finished version of the first part, the

Siena days. Unhappily, it is incomplete, but it is instructive to see how Dunne stylistically "improved" it, perhaps for publication.

The next items are two related articles, of which the first is quite definitely a finished piece meant for publication. At the top of it is written: "Submitted by Brian Ború Dunne," and evidently this or the two articles together constitute the "article" he mentioned to Wells in 1935, meant for publication in the London *Times*. In the headnote, however, we adduce some evidence that it may have been written later, but it seems unlikely that it was ever submitted—at least there are no editorial marks on either manuscript, nor any evidence that an editor had read them, and they certainly contain none of Orage's requests.

These two items are followed by extracts taken from Dunne's very long and engaging memoir of Senator Bronson Cutting. Almost certainly they reflect the spirit of the evenings spent with Cutting in his illness, during which Dunne recounted the seemingly endless stories of Gissing in the Italian days. These appear to have been written in a more spontaneous mood, with little of the conscious journalistic overlay we occasionally sense in the other documents. Partly for this reason we have added in appendices two of Dunne's journalistic pieces, one on Cardinal Gibbons, the other on William Jennings Bryan. These, we think, are not only interesting in themselves, but also reflect the personality and the style of the man who wrote the memoirs of Gissing. By the time he wrote them he had been a journalist all his adult life, and the memoirs should be read with that in mind.

For all his varied achievements, Dunne seems to us a man who did not take himself with deadly seriousness, and certainly he was blessed with a very lively sense of humor. He employed that sense of humor most deliberately in his first book, *Cured!* and in discussing it above we described it as somewhat exaggerated, written in the style of American humor near the turn of the century, when he was probably influenced by the personality and the work of Mark Twain. In the memoirs, however, the humor is far from intrusive, and it is most evident when the stories center on himself as well as on Gissing. And in fact it is Dunne's presence in the memoirs that accounts to a very large extent for their vitality and, indeed, for their unique importance to us. For these are memoirs not only of Gissing, but of Dunne *with* Gissing, and in this exchange between personalities we see a portrait of Gissing which no one else has been able to give us. In Gabrielle Fleury's memoir (see *Collected Letters,* vol. 9), which for its range and its concentration on Gissing is obviously a very different record, Gabrielle is also there, but almost never is she a real, felt presence. She is perforce the narrator, she does say where "we" went and whom "we" met, and she does ask an occasional question and record snippets of conversation. But except when she is describing Gissing's death she rarely reveals her own feelings or expresses an opinion, and so her presence there is nearly always a mere fact. Dunne was no cipher, however, and while at times it may seem that his self is there partially to satisfy his ego, yet it was that ego which drew out the response of Gissing, and doubtless it was his instinct as a journalist that urged him to describe not only the words of Gissing but also the causes and occasions of them. Even his account of the long quest for tickets to a papal mass, in which Dunne seems to be carried away by his own adventures with princes and cardinals, reveals itself ultimately as a story about Gissing as well as about Dunne—these episodes, after all, are what Gissing himself knew about Dunne, and when we are admitted into the scene we are reminded that these two led independent lives even in Rome, that Gissing's personality occasioned the hunt while Dunne's gave him the energy to pursue it, and that the ardor of Gissing's interest and the few glimpses we get of his arch and witty responses tell us as much about Gissing as the frankness of narrative tells us about the proud and modest Dunne. As always, the irony and good humor are there. Having hoped only for tickets to a mass in St. Peter's, the largest cathedral in the world, he ends up with rarer tickets to the smaller Sistine Chapel, but he says not a word about that—it is for us to get the point. Even the incredible final episode with the German baroness, whom Dunne says he had met in his boardinghouse, is nevertheless credible because everything else Dunne says is credible. The final paragraph is a tactical and stylistic gem. It ends with her blessing on Gissing's soul in his illness, as if he were headed for the grave, and we are made to realize that even this tiny episode was occasioned by Gissing.

There is one other important factor to be kept in mind when reading these memoirs, and that is the relative disparity in what Gissing and Dunne knew of each other. It is clear enough from the absence of details in the memoirs themselves that Gissing was quite silent about his private life, but direct and positive evidence of that is in the final entry of Dunne's list of topics: "Never talked of '*my wife*.'" It was a topic Gissing was not likely to talk of, and quite certainly the more sordid conditions of Gissing's private life were not details which Dunne neglected out of a sense of delicacy, but details he never knew. As to Gissing's "wife," one might think that any kind of intellectual work is hardly possible without mental as well as physical peace, and Gissing's capacity to produce literary work with women like Nell and Edith, his successive wives, in his modest living quarters, seems little short of a miracle. And it is equally extraordinary that he could write a book like *Charles Dickens: A Critical Study* under the unsettling conditions of a lodging house, and in a foreign country at that, and especially at a time when he feared that serious work might have become impossible for him. While he was at his desk (or rather, at *any* desk) his capacity for mental concentration was indeed impressive, but doubtless a good deal of that depended on a rigid schedule. When Gissing arrived in Italy, he did have a set schedule in mind: write during the day, and relax in the evening. But loneliness was not conducive to work either, and an unexpected gift from Fortune was the appearance of Brian Dunne, an engaging youth, brimful of curiosity and eagerness to learn, and of unbounded friendliness. In his company, Gissing seems to have developed a new persona. Although Dunne had never heard of him and was unconditioned by any reading of his novels, he may have learned that Gissing was a famous writer, but he personally observed him as a classical scholar, an excellent conversationalist, a witty companion, and an elegantly prepared so-journer in Italy. Gissing used the national trait of reticence to ad-vantage: Dunne was aware that, like the American Indian, the English preferred to be what they were at the moment—personal infor-mation was not given nor even offered—and Gissing struck him as very, very English indeed. Gissing with Dunne was another man, a personality that showed what brilliance of character and charm might have existed had his life not taken that cursed step with Nell Harrison in his student days.

And Dunne was something else. He struck Gissing as very, very American, and Gissing must have had a pretty clear idea of the social environment in which young Brian had lived in America. He certainly knew a good deal about his opinions—social, cultural, re-ligious; he knew the kind of people with whom Brian had associ-ated in the United States as well as in Europe, and doubtless too he knew about Brian's father, the colony in which he had been raised, his school studies, and even the family itself. But Brian was also a student, who must have brought back to Gissing those invigorating days when he was a young tutor to such boys as the Harrisons and the various relatives of no less than four dukes. From what we have learned of Gissing as a teacher, he seems to have been remarkably impressive: his students liked him and respected him, and their later successes confirmed his efforts. Dunne was the perfect student for a tutor at the age of forty: intelligent, rather sophisticated in some ways, and overjoyed to be in the company of an intellectually and artistically accomplished older man—more friend than teacher, more equal companion than academic guide, but nonetheless in-herently a teacher. Dunne did not stress this part of the relation-ship, but it is implicit nearly everywhere in the memoirs, and it is what is meant by the claim that he "studied under" Gissing.

It seems to us that the forthright and congenial spirit reflected in these memoirs captures the spirit of the experiences them-selves, and because of it we are more comfortable in accepting the authenticity of the account. Dunne had a keen eye for concrete de-tails, and unlike in other memoirs we learn here a good deal about

Gissing from small things—his daily ritual baths, his dread of getting his head wet while taking one, his screaming down the stairs of a bathless pension, his shyness and his blushing, his bragging response to the American disdain for English "properness," his dinners in small restaurants with an occasional foray into the "swell" ones, his exorbitant love of Italian cakes, his animated disgust for scarlet women, his acid criticisms of nations and peoples (but always in good taste), his amusement at human folly—and all this told, often in a style whose sparseness stresses details, by a man who not only tells us about himself but confesses his own ignorance, his foibles, and his desire to impress others: "I wanted him to think me grand," Dunne says of Cardinal del Val. In these pages we see and hear Gissing as he was in daily life during those months in Italy, and Dunne gives us a portrait that is unequaled. He wanted us to see how happy a time this was for Gissing, and we think we understand why it was so. But we also see occasionally a Gissing who was maturing in judgment, and no longer quite the blind worshiper of the Romans that Wells said he was: coming out of the Forum, in a fit of anger, he exclaims "After all, those Romans were a bloodthirsty lot!" And no one, after reading these memoirs, can ever again hold the view that Gissing was a man without a sense of humor.

In choosing to print all the versions here, we are well aware of the repetitive aspect, which some readers may find annoying, but the full effect can be felt only from the whole of them, not from a composite memoir composed of sections from each document. Certainly the same stories are told more than once, but the variations in the telling are instructive. Most often what Dunne adds or alters is an attempt to recapture the mood of the moment, and perhaps to enhance the dramatic effect, but it should be noted that in no case is there an essential or substantial alteration. According to his son, he wrote his memoirs in a reflective, meditative mood, and they simply record his different states of mind. One of Dunne's journalistic virtues seems to be truthfulness, and that is one reason we have given so much attention to him here. While this is by definition and intention a book about Gissing, the subject of the memoirs, it has also rather strangely developed into a book about the man who wrote them. BrianBorú Dunne seems to us to have been a man whose life, personality, and family deserve to be memorialized in some way, and we are well pleased to have had the occasion to do it briefly here. We are indebted to his son, Brian B. Dunne, who, in his long career as a physicist, is probably best known for leading the experimental group that designed and flight-tested the Project Orion meter model presently on exhibit in the Smithsonian Air and Space Museum. His patient efforts in searching through the vast quantities of his father's papers, his remarkable memory and literary knowledge, and his forthright willingness to cooperate at every stage of this project have been an indispensable aid, and have helped to make the labor of editing a congenial enterprise.

Memoirs

MS-A

The Memoir

[THE DUNNE MEMOIRS of Gissing consist of six items, two (MSS-C and -D) in the form of articles meant for publication in journals. Then there is a collection of anecdotes taken from Dunne's memoirs of his close friend Senator Bronson Cutting (MS-E), followed by a list of topics (MS-F) from which he drew when writing the actual memoirs. The first item, "Personal Recollections of George Gissing" (MS-A), followed by a revision of part of it (MS-B), is the longest document, evidently intended as a book. It is typed on fifty-two pages of standard typing paper, which we have pieced together from three yellowing and crumbling copies, so that nothing is missing in the version we present here. It seems to be a first draft, not a "finished" product ready for submission to a publisher, although the foreword seems to mean that Dunne had the book form of publication in mind. The fact that he puts in certain directions or reminders to himself, such as an indication of subheadings, or the notation that "this is the end of the first batch," suggests that the content as well as the form itself may not have been final. And in fact the many lines between paragraphs, which convey a lack of any deliberate order, give the impression that this was not so much a first draft as a preliminary expansion of episodes taken from the list of topics (see MS-F). That list, however, cannot be dated. Perhaps Dunne also drew on it in writing the later articles, but since some episodes in them are also included here, it seems likely that the list was drawn up prior to any writing at all. The fact that he expanded some episodes even further when he used them for the more finished articles does not mean that he altered the substance, but rendered the episodes more complete, sometimes even attempting to recapture, in a journalistic way, the state of mind or emotion at the time they occurred. Since the memoir was never published, and since it contains relatively few of the topics on the long list, it seems clear that Dunne set aside the project before he finished it. He did enter several corrections and additions here in brown ink, but made no attempt to correct typographic or other errors, even when they are factual. For example, the name of Dickens's biographer seems to have momentarily eluded him, but rather than interrupt his writing he substituted a name at hand, de Forrest, evidently the Civil War novelist John William de Forest, author of *Miss Ravenel's Conversion* (1866). This confirms our view that this is a preliminary draft: since he got Forster's name right in the revision which follows it and in the other articles, we may presume that he would have made such corrections in a draft prepared for publication. All of this may suggest that the memoir was written in that kind of haste, and so it manages to convey a greater sense of spontaneity. We have corrected a few of these errors, along with the typos, whenever it seemed appropriate. We present the memoir here as first in the order of composition, not only because it is the longest, but also because Dunne expressed to H. G. Wells his intention to write it in 1933, and only in 1935 did he mention an article. In the documentation, we have at times repeated some information from the introduction, not to satisfy any subtle theory of redundancy, but for the sake of readers who will read the memoirs before the introduction, or even in place of it.]

Personal Recollections of George Gissing
By Brian Ború Dunne

Foreword.—I am writing these reminiscences of George Gissing, perhaps a great literary man,[1] principally for the amusement and instruction of young writers, and for the diversion of Gissing fans the world over—and people in all the English speaking countries and also in France had read Gissing. Many of them have written to Gissing. . . , and found a certain comfort in his struggle up the literary ladder, his sufferings, his remarkable courage.[2]— The Author.

I first met Gissing in a boarding house in Siena, Italy. He was then at his prime, as some would call it—forty years of age, full of "pep" as we Americans say, and loaded with ambition. He was a tall Englishman, with long brown-reddish hair combed back, clear blue eyes and rather pale complexion.

He had a habit—or valvular weakness—of blushing like a school girl when he was contradicted, or when some unpleasant memory was brought up by a direct question. I never saw in my 35 years of newspaper reporting any human being blush more violently than Gissing when I, only 19 years of age, and an ardent Irishman, asked him this question: "What is the matter with Ireland? Why in the world has that country been held back? What has Ireland done to England to get this treatment?"

I well remember his reply: "There is something wrong, terribly wrong about it all." And he appeared nearly suffocated, and I vowed never again to bring up the subject.[3] But it came up later on—in a sermon by Cardinal Parocchi in Rome[4]—every word of which Gissing asked me to repeat to him in the presence of H. G. Wells.

When I met Gissing he was one of those English inhabitants of a Continental *pension,* as they call it, who was a mystery to his own landlady in that he never spoke to anyone except at meals.[5]

I had gone to Europe at the age of 17 years to study principally the German language—conversational German—and I was to live in the homes of peasants to acquire their dialect to assist my father in a colony or land project in Florida.[6] My father had decided the Germans were the best gardeners in the world, and the most industrious people (with the French), and they would be the ideal race to extract dollars from the sandy soil of Florida. They could raise oranges and strawberries, and become happy in a new land of opportunity. Germany was crowded or over-crowded, and a banker named Cahensly wrote my father: "We are increasing at 800,000 a year and must send emigrants to America."[7]

When I met Gissing I had spent five months in Belgium studying French and a year in Germany. I had done 1500 hours in French and 3,000 hours in German. I had studied English, Latin and Greek in America.

Gissing became interested in me when he discovered that I studied Horace every night[8]—instead of joining the Italian students at the boarding house or pension in games of "shooting pool"—which seemed to be the chief diversion in quiet, classic, lazy Siena. Later I learned that Gissing was interested in men who had studied and starved, and who liked Latin and Greek—and who minded their own business by not asking personal questions.[9] (This is the rule of cultured Englishmen and American Indians, I also have discovered.)

It took about three days to get an invitation from Gissing to visit him in his room at the pension and discuss literature. Then one night he told me he was a writer.

Frankly, I had never heard of him or of Kipling—for my education was in the year 1897 very much confined to high school studies and travel—and a few Continental languages.

And soon I discovered I had met a literary slave—enduring a form of slavery which seemed to Gissing as terrible as that of rowing in a galley for a Roman task-master, with an awful "view ahead."

Gissing started his day's work of writing at 9 A.M. and plodded until noon. Then we would see him emerge from the room with the high ceiling which was his apartment, and he was red in the face from mental activity. We took an hour, Italian custom, to lunch on the delightful food of a Sienese boarding house with a glass or two of *Chianti* to help digestion. And back he went to work until late in the afternoon when he would take a walk—often inviting me to join him. All Englishmen walk—even in this day of motor cars.

And in the evening Gissing would talk for an hour or two and then go to bed to read books—and books that came in the mails. And this was six days in the week, but on Sundays there was a day of rest. All English men seem to rest on Sundays except the bus drivers of London.

Gissing told me his troubles. He had signed a contract—and I gather he sealed it with a down payment—to write "*Charles Dickens*—a critical study"—volume of 80,000 words. And he had to complete it in a given time and he received letters, I think, reminding him of that *awful day*—the deadline day.[10] How he struggled.

Gissing said that on this type of work, a critical study, he could not do more than a thousand words a day. About 6,000 a week.

His Method of Work (sub)

It may interest writers, particularly young writers and Gissing admirers, to know his method of work. He would do all of his day's writing, of 1,000 words, on one large sheet of paper. And he wrote with a pen, and as far as I could ascertain he never struck out a word or changed a comma.[11] An extraordinary person.

What amazed me one morning when I saw Gissing at work— I delivered a letter to him—was the discovery that Gissing travelled without a dictionary of the English language. He had a dress suit, in case of an invitation to dine; he had even a rubber bath tub, for no Englishman could go without daily bath, and Siena boarding houses had no tubs.

The only book he used apparently to assist in that splendid work on Dickens was Forster's Life of Dickens—a massive volume bound in green cloth.[12]

Gissing, of course, knew a lot about Dickens before he started to eat and digest Forster's Life. And no doubt he had read every book by Dickens.

Every night Gissing exclaimed—after a fearful day's work— "This is a terrible thing—this contract."

One day I made an injudicious reference to Forster's Life, into which I peeked at times—when the day's battle was over. I noticed that Forster had published a letter from Dickens about the habit of American travelers of spitting on the marble floors of hotel lobbies. I need not mention the exact description given by Dickens. Gissing remarked: "I have read that—and for two years I have tried to forget it."[13]

It was disgusting—and quite unnecessary. But Dickens had that terrible gift of picturing on paper what he saw. During his work of studying Dickens and his writings and his life, Gissing would boil over with indignation. His chief and perhaps only grievance against Dickens was the American tour. "If he had stayed at home and avoided that tiresome lecture tour, he would be living today." This was his comment.

Dickens had some asthmatic trouble—I gathered—and yet he went on lecturing—for money and more money.[14]

As to his method of work. Gissing said that in writing novels, he could do much more than 1,000 words in 8 hours. An Italian newspaper arrived telling of a successful Italian novelist who did a good (or best?) seller in six weeks, who worked 10 hours a day living entirely on fruit. This novelist explained: "I write my last chapters and then go toward the beginning and see what I have to do."[15] Gissing said: "I do not work that way. I know everything I am going to do when I write a novel. I have all the characters before me, and I proceed from the first chapter on to the end of the novel."

I had spent a vacation with Belgian classmates at their chateau in Northern France. They were princes. Their mother was of English and Irish blood. Their sister, who became famous in the *World War*,[16] used to tease me about America and Americans because of what Dickens wrote—when he was unable to get a copyright to protect him on sales of his books in America.[17] As everyone knows, Dickens did not spare the weakness of Americans.

I remonstrated with Gissing, declaring that Dickens had not painted a fair picture of Americans. "But that period was years ago," he replied.

Gissing was fascinated with the declaration of the princess that Dickens' "masterpiece," "Pickwick Papers," was coarse. "Women think Dickens coarse, I suppose," he replied with a sneer. I think he mentioned this point in his critical study.[18]

As Gissing continued his work on Dickens, it was evident that the English Superiority was always in Gissing's mind. Every nation came forward as a poor second. *Great England*.[19] It was evident, too, that Gissing had travelled all over Europe, and had read of every country in the world, and had met many foreigners. Literary recluse as he has been called, he saw a lot of the world.

In the evening Gissing discussed the weakness of various people, and he had sarcastic remarks about the French, and the Germans, and the Greeks, and the Italians. No nation in the world, perhaps, amused him so much as the Italians. After all, they are quite different from the cold, diffident, supremely efficient English. And Gissing said things about the Americans, too, for he had lived in the U.S.A.[20]

His Conversation. (sub)

In his conversation, covering a period of nearly a year,[21] during various hours of the day and night, I never heard Gissing use:

A damn.

A hell.

An immodest word.

His vocabulary was so large, so magnificent, he found no need of [one line missing in surviving copy]. Once Gissing seemed to find the language of Shakespeare and Dickens inadequate, and he remarked about some tomfoolery of Italian officials: "They are using what you in America call *red tape,*" he said.[22]

Once Gissing narrated what he considered a terrible story of a brother Englishman "trapped" on the Island of Capri by a luscious Italian maiden. "In plain language," he began, with the air of a physician discussing some unpleasant malady, "he seduced that girl." Gissing seemed to think it improper to use the word *seduce.*[23]

Gissing loved to discuss words stolen by the English language from a foreign tongue. He gave me a lecture on the word *Bosh*—which he said came from the Turkish or Persian—I forget which. And he explained that the word was offensive to *Turks*—but in English, it was a common word, an exclamation of power. It was expressive.[24]

And this lecture on the word *Bosh* led to an unpleasant incident
—almost to murder.

One night, after Gissing had finished his splendid book on
Charles Dickens, we found ourselves in *Rome* (Roma Immortalis).[25]
Gissing then was preparing, through research in libraries, for his
work "By the Ionian Sea" or some such name.[26] And after dining at
Fiorelli's on the Corso,[27] we followed the Italian custom of sipping
a demi tasse of (rather vile) black coffee in an Italian cafe. I remember it was brilliantly lighted. All went well, this charming man
sipping coffee with great gusto and discussing the time of Julius
Caesar, until a "terrible looking Turk" entered the cafe. He carried
Oriental rugs, the bright colors nearly blinding my eyes in the brilliantly lighted cafe.

Seeing the Turk I was overcome with a terrible desire to speak
Turkish—and I remembered the one word *Bosh*. I was quite young,
and wished to see whether Gissing had the "low down" on the
power of that word to enrage Turks. So I looked at the rugs offered
me—us—for sale and exclaimed *Bosh*. The Turk glared. I repeated
it. Gissing became livid and exclaimed something about "getting out
of here." The Turk gave me more than a menacing look—there was
a dagger-pulling gesture. The proprietor of the cafe, sensing trouble, dashed forward and the Turk, still glaring, retreated. Gissing
spilt his cup of coffee in the saucer and all over the marble-topped
table. He beckoned me to leave the cafe with him. "Why did you do
that?" he asked with a look more of horror than of rage. "I wished
to see how it sounded in a Turk's ears," I replied innocently. "I never
knew before how to enrage a Turk. You taught me in Siena." Gissing
walked to his rooming house, where I left him. He walked in silence. It was evident I had displeased him—somewhat.

(This is the end of the first batch)
b.b.d.

We next take up Mr Gissing's remarks about the Italians and Italy.

Gissing and the Italians.

All during Gissing's sojourn in Italy, covering a period of nearly a year, it became more and more evident that this English writer found this land of lovely monuments and smiling women, of gorgeous groves and vineyards and beautiful colors, one grand, rollicking circus.

To understand how Gissing got this impression one must remember he had just come from London, the largest city in the world, and in many ways the most efficiently built, managed, controlled, directed and operated. There are slums and poor in London but they are not right up against the beautiful parks and grand avenues. An American newspaperman visits London and finds there is no "monkey business," as in the Italy of Gissing's day. By monkey business he will mean the hanging of wet clothes out of a window, dripping on pedestrians in the street below. In London if a motor car today has a gash in a fender, a bobby will call the taxi driver to see that it is repaired immediately, for this gash in the metal may cause a gash in some important Englishman's coat. In London the owners of property are as considerate of their beautifully carved front doors as they are of their pet horses. Both must have a canvas shield or curtain or bonnet from the summer sun. It is a common sight to see curtains drawn over the wooden doors during the hours sun shines on them. Not so in Italy. London simply oozes with efficiency, just as the Englishman of any education is always well turned out—well dressed. He has to be fit in body, in mind and—and in appearance. The Italians of Gissing's day seemed to do as they damned please, and dress as they damned please, to use the American slang. All this proved a rollicking circus, a three tent show to Gissing, who yearned to leave his library or his room, where he toiled over manuscripts, to enjoy the fun, full details of which he narrated to me at meals, during our promenades and at night when we conversed about the day's happenings.

The thing that most amused Gissing was the Italian rooming houses where there were no baths. "*Non c'è*" was the answer often given when Gissing and I hunted rooms and asked about the most important room in the house.

When informed that there was no bath room convenience in the house, Gissing would smile faintly and politely bid addio to the landlady or landlord, who looked puzzled at the Englishman's evident desire to dash out of the door and down the stairs. And Gissing would scream as he ran down the stairs.

Another thing that amused Gissing was his landlord's desire to "fete" him—for he finally got a landlord who had a bath room. On important festivals, especially Christmas and New Year's, the Englishman, always called "Signor Giorgio," was expected to dine with the landlord. The sumptuous meal, which appalled even an Englishman's appetite, was topped off with fruits and puddings and cakes, and then a big plate piled high with cheap candy. Gissing said he was expected to eat all that stuff.[28]

Gissing was also convulsed by the Italian custom of travellers getting off trains, dashing into depots, and emerging with various items of clothing unbuttoned. He would have been more shocked to travel on a Japanese train today and see the Japs change an entire suit of clothes in the main aisle.[29]

The conversation at the boarding house or pension in Siena with all Italians as the guests—except Gissing and me—bowled the English writer over—and over. Cappelli, an Italian medical student, sent Gissing into convulsions by declaring that the newspapers were all wrong about the brigands arrested in Sicily being Dante scholars. Cappelli said that the presence of copies of Dante in the pockets of the brigands did not mean they read and admired Dante. Cappelli went into details and Gissing remarked to me: "The young man went a trifle far—for dinner conversation."[30]

Gissing could not understand why the authorities of the city of Rome permitted Italians to walk around the streets at 2, 3, 4 o'clock in the morning singing in good but tenor voices. "This is a large city and I suppose some of these men are having affairs," he remarked. As Ruggles would say: "This would not do with us, sir."[31] One night an Italian singer, with a magnificent voice, did a serenade in front of Gissing's boarding house on the Via Panisperna, near the Roman Forum.[32] He sang for about an hour and no police interrupted. He was a trifle tight, no doubt.

Gissing and I usually dined in a cheap restaurant frequented by writers and artists. But on occasion, perhaps after signing a contract for a new book, Gissing would blow himself to a so-called swell restaurant and pay double prices. But he reaped his reward. He always had a "scream of a story." A gayly dressed party of young men and women had taken a table near him; the men in full dress, the women in velvets and pearls. The leader of the party, an Italian count, gave the orders and in a loud voice told the waiter to cook the omelet for his wife, a beautiful dame with an unusually spacious bosom, in butter "because my wife is *enceinte.*" Gissing said the Italian nobleman had said in a loud voice "*Poiché la mia moglie è incinta.*"[33]

Gissing nearly choked, but no one else paid any attention—the waiter merely bowing. I told Gissing I had heard the Latins and the Germans were proud of pregnant wives—as they should be. "I see no reason for advertising it all over the restaurant," replied Gissing in defense. Of course, they would not do that in London. The English are particular about what they say.

Gissing said that one of the most amusing experiences he had had in Italy or in his life on New Year's eve was in Florence in the early '90s when he was dining quietly in a restaurant. As the New Year was welcomed with a few guns and city bells, every Italian man in the restaurant appeared to go insane and rang every bell in the restaurant, struck champagne glasses with knives, forks and spoons, and whistled shrilly. One Italian pushed Gissing almost out of his chair to grab a braided silk cord in the corner—it rang a bell out in the kitchen.[34]

The signs in the streets amused Gissing—and sometimes we

missed a street car or bus while he read them and expounded on their stupidity. Over a restaurant near the Piazza di Spagna in Rome was this lovely announcement: "*Aperto fino alle ore inoltrate.*" Gissing said it twice aloud and remarked: "Fools—that means open to unheard of hours and no restaurant could be open to unheard of hours."[35]

The presence of Italian soldiers in their neat little uniforms—and the uniforms were little to fit the men—and the white spats, drove Gissing into convulsions. At times he came out of those convulsions to remark: "All this military preparedness of Italy in a triple alliance with Germany and Austria is the height of absurdity. It is like a boy trying to walk with a tall man—trying to keep up with an adult."[36] Every time Gissing read or heard of that Triple Alliance he scowled.

The sale of contraceptives on the street corners of the large cities and the flood of scarlet women let loose exactly at the noon hour up and down the Corso, Rome's famous business and social thoroughfare, angered Gissing. Americans I talked to were first aghast and then amused. Gissing hated the name, the thought, the presence, the descriptions, the suggestion of prostitution, which was gaily discussed by Latins at luncheon. The subject of Gissing and scarlet women will be treated in another chapter.

On every occasion when Italy and the Italians were subjects of discussion, the Englishman's superiority of an Englishman cropped out. The Italian tailors were bum. They made a dress suit —so essential in Rome for the Pope's Mass at the Vatican—about half as good as the London brand. I always had heard London made the best clothes in the world. The Italian valises or bags were of poor leather—London turned out the finest leather in the world. Gissing would not even mention Russian leather in the same breath.

There was one thing Gissing believed the Italians surpassed Europe in—the making of cakes. And he ate a cake, a whole cake, whenever he could afford it and he bragged of his extravagance. These cakes were marvelous.

The Italian libraries where Gissing often worked were well stocked with valuable books, well lighted and clean, but the management was a joke. So Gissing found. An Italian library manager angered and humiliated Gissing by rebuking him for reading a newspaper in the library.[37] Gissing had finished some research work and took a peek into the daily *Tribuna* to see what the king was doing that day.

The libraries, furnishing free books as well as free desk room and free heat in winter, appealed to Gissing as to other poor writers and students. Gissing said that in London a student would be let alone in the libraries, but even England had to draw the line on the use of the library wash basin as a bath tub. He said that some of the people who visited the London libraries used the institution not only for mental but also for bodily development—that they went down to the lavatory and stripped to the waist and washed their arms and bodies. A sign was put up about "Gentlemen are requested to use this lavatory for the ablution of face and hands." I cannot recall the exact wording but it was in fine English and Gissing chuckled as he recalled it.[38] At the same time Gissing said he thought the Italian library managers went a trifle far in rebuking a writer for peeping into a newspaper.

The King (Umberto) like everyone else in Rome amused Gissing.

Poor Umberto, grayhaired, with enormous black eyes blazing like coals of fire, and the fierce mustachios, often drove through the streets. This brave monarch, as history tells, was mowed down by an assassin's bullet. The king felt it his duty to show himself to his people and apparently never wore a bullet proof vest. Maybe like Napoleon after Moscow he courted a cannon ball.[39]

I liked to look into Umberto's eyes and found that the way to get Umberto to look intently at you was to stand on the street corner as he drove by in his gorgeous carriage drawn by two fiery black steeds, and fail to salute him. This may have seemed rude but, after all, an American tourist might not have recognized him as His Majesty. On one occasion I did this of a late afternoon and Umberto peered into my eyes—in wonder perhaps. It was rumored in ecclesiastical circles none too friendly to Umberto that the king "scraped for recognition." Perhaps he felt he was unpopular.[40]

Umberto's eyes were bloodshot. I told Gissing and he chuckled: "The old boy was out late last night. A grand drinking party, eh?"

As Gissing remained in Rome, England heard about his visit and prominent English women invited him to tea, and Gissing went —occasionally, coming home with a lot of gossip.[41] Rome was, indeed, a mere village, as far as gossip was concerned.

One of the stories was that a beautiful lady-in-waiting from Naples had flirted outrageously with gray-haired Umberto at a ball and Queen Marguerite finally dismissed her by saying "Madame, I think it would benefit your health to take a vacation at home." And the lady-in-waiting had replied: "I am ready to leave, Your Majesty, now that your consort has paid all my debts."

Gissing met a bright and handsome young English journalist who lived in Rome and who sent dispatches to the London *Mail.* Gissing said that [Roman] monsignori—minor prelates, but wearers of the purple—actually called on this young man, carrying parcels of news from the Vatican. This was too much for Gissing. A mere journalist getting such attention![42]

But even bishops, lords of their domain, are minor dignitaries in the city of a pope and many cardinals.

Gissing could not understand how the Italian restaurant owners would tolerate the custom he witnessed of guests—Italians—
ordering a glass of wine and then having it filled up at least ¾ and
calling it half a glass.

Gissing would sneak into a tiny restaurant off the Corso and
take me with him just for one purpose—to see the 60 year old Italian gentleman "pull" that trick, remarking: "That man is the perfect
image of my publisher, old Bullen."[43] Every time the Italian called
to a waiter to fill his glass not quite drained, Gissing would chuckle
"Old Bullen is pulling down another drink."

Gissing sized up the Italians as a bunch of children. But this
was years before Mussolini took over Italy and made it into a Ger-
man-like machine. Mussolini evidently stopped a lot of this "monkey business" in Rome—at noon today the scarlet women no longer
flaunt their smiles and sparkling eyes on rich-looking foreigners
along the Corso.

The "Cafés Chantants" certainly amused me—as I had never
been to such places. Only once could I get Gissing into one, but we
had a marvelous evening. A girl called "Stella"—of course pretty
and full bosomed—sang and danced and created a furor. She was
given a dozen encores and then the orchestra leader decided that
enough was enough. To repeated cries, particularly from an upper
box to the right of the stage, that Stella reappear, there was silence.
Screams of *"Fuori la Stella"* were uttered by a half dozen slightly
drunken young men. Still Stella failed to shine. Finally the uproar
became so great Stella appeared and was showered with cigarettes,
walnuts, peanuts, carnations, cigars, marbles, spitballs and what not.
The orchestra leader gave a signal and the curtain was rung down
and the crowd dispersed.

I thought the orchestra delightful and I loved their gay tunes, but Gissing remarked: "These musicians are working for seven francs a week." He was most sarcastic. But he thought the Italians' reception of Stella highly amusing.[44]

Gissing disapproved of this cafe chantant amusement—so popular with the Italian youth of Rome—as a waste of time. Moreover, a whole troupe of scarlet women were reported to infest these places, entering without paying admission fees, and luring the men to buy drinks.

Gissing and Climate

It has been remarked by the editors of *Gissing's Letters* (a volume that sold for the large sum of six dollars) that the English writer had an amazing habit of writing constantly about the weather.[45] This was one of Gissing's faults, and may have been due to the effect of climate upon his frail health. At the age of forty Gissing may have developed tuberculosis, which he called phthisis. (Trust the English to pick out a nice word for anything unpleasant.)

While England to Gissing was God's paradise on earth, with London the perfect city and its inhabitants the super-human-beings of this globe, Gissing was tactfully silent about the London climate until he discussed a London fog. And then he talked for an hour. The climate of Italy was delightful, at least in winter, and certainly was superior to that of London. Gissing's test of an ideal day in January was to go to a park like the Pincio and light a match. If the match did not blow out that was an ideal weather condition for the meteorologists to rave about.

As to a real fog in London, Gissing would describe it like Jules Verne would describe a maelstrom in "20,000 Leagues Under the Sea." It took about an hour for Gissing to tell all about it. Pedestrians had to cling *to* the sidewalk to *find* the sidewalk. A real smart Englishman actually became bewildered once in his life. He could die in battle with a smile or sink on a battleship with a grin, but in a London fog he was lost a-foot, a-horseback or in a cab. It was terrible.

Curious Customs in England

While all Italy was a holy show, a circus or a menagerie to Gissing, the English writer in moments of weakness would admit that there were a few curious customs in London, the city perfect, inhabited by mastermen and proper women.

One of these customs Gissing narrated one night in Siena when he delivered his most bitter invective against scarlet women roaming the world to produce physical, moral and financial ruin to their stronger brethren called *men.*

According to Gissing this was not merely a rude adventure thrust upon the worthy admirers of the drama and the opera, but a veritable battle in which more than one cultured Englishman found his clothes torn or rumpled, and his hat knocked off or crushed. It was disgusting. And nothing was done about it.

Another custom connected with the theatre but more amusing than disgusting was that of an elderly English Lord whose name I cannot recall, for I am writing from memory after a period of 38 years. This English Lord was not handsome nor young but he was rich, of course. And he liked to get a "kick" out of the commotion he caused among hack drivers (cabbies) by always giving a guinea for a ride, no matter how short the ride.

As a result every cabby *fought* over the frail body of His Lordship, who enjoyed the scrabble he caused by his little extravagance. Of course the fare was a shilling or two, but the nobleman paid out the five dollars, or guinea. Whenever the nobleman appeared leaving a theater, the cabbies forgot all other "fares" and besieged him with shouts of *"This way my lord"* and *"Oh my lord this way."*

Gissing and Physicians

The London physicians at home and the English physicians abroad were, like all Englishmen to Gissing, the supermen of their profession, as they should be.[46] An Englishman is carefully educated —with boarding houses for youngsters of the age of eight and then on. And the Englishman, be he at the bar of so-called justice, or in the laboratory, or at sea, or in battle, knows his "stuff."

As for the Italian physicians, Gissing considered them huge jokes. He said that when he was nearly dying of a fever on his tour of Southern Italy to get material for *By the Ionian Sea,* his doctor tried to ram beefsteak and pour wine down his throat. As Gissing, thanks to nature, climbed out of the fever and began to ascend the ladder of health, the doctor exclaimed with a magnificent gesture: *"No food, Signor."*[47]

Like every other Italian, the medico was a child, according to Gissing.

But Gissing, in a moment of absentmindedness or weakness, told a wicked story on an English physician he encountered in Verona.[48] Gissing got a cinder in his eye and dashed to the *English* physician in the city. Gissing's livelihood depended on his eyes. The English physician promptly extracted the cinder and, forgetting that he was dealing with a poor writer, murmured *"The fee will be a guinea d'or."* Gissing considered the fee outrageously high for the small effort of extracting a tiny cinder, and the murmuring of a guinea d'or an added outrage.

A London physician and writer, a Gissing fan, hearing this story, said to me: "He charged a guinea d'or? Good for him."

The charges of the Italian physician, like all charges in Italy in 1898, were modest. And the Italian physician, like all Italians, was polite, sympathetic and charming.[49]

Gissing and Appearance

Gissing had the correct Englishman's view that every gentleman should take a full bath every day—and he jeered at Italians who said a sponge bath was good enough. If there is no bath tub in Rome, or in Siena, in the wilds of India or Africa, the Englishman must carry a rubber tub. And the gentleman must shave every day. And keep his hair reasonably short.

Gissing was *wild* at Hall Caine (famous for *The Christian*) for walking around Rome in a golf suit and with waving long hair. He called him some awful name.[50]

As to shirts, an Englishman must never be seen in a city where there are English with a flannel shirt on—that is for the bicycle tour or hike. Once Gissing was accosted by a prominent London society man in the Piazza di Spagna, and Gissing told me of the awful experience. The Londoner was sure to consider Gissing a hick—from then on.[51]

Gissing had the usual Englishman's idea of the "white man" supremacy in foreign colonies.

There was one undignified act an Englishman in a foreign possession like India might do—and that is, go mad, according to Gissing. Instead of deploring the act, Gissing praised Kipling for describing an English army officer gradually going mad from the climate and solitude in India. (I do not know in which story this description appears, but Gissing pronounced it marvelous.)[52]

The *most gracious* act of an Englishman that Gissing recalled —at least in conversations with me—was that of an English Lord who had gone to Rome to realize a dream of "grandeur"—some Arabian Nights stuff. This Lord rented a huge apartment, employed a brilliant English young man as secretary and society assistant, and proceeded to entertain lavishly. His gracious act was to serve a great dinner, with a fine wine at each course, and then top off the meal with rare vintages (costing $1 a spoonful) taken out of a huge gold bottle with a revolving door. The key to his bottle (the size of a magnum champagne), was kept in the right vest pocket of an English nobleman. It was a tiny key for a tiny lock in the mysterious bottle. Gissing was invited repeatedly to dine with this English Lord —Gissing had outlived or mastered Grub Street and starvation— and now was dining and wining and champagning with England's most important people. The dinners were superb, but Gissing, most sensitive of human beings and also one of the most romantic, re-marked that some of the courses were a trifle cold, and the wine or wines were welcome. The meals were brought to the Lord's apart-ment in huge tin boxes from a famous hotel. Another Italian cus-tom, but it gave the host an opportunity to entertain with meals of splendor, without hiring a chef and a retinue of assistant cooks. Some more English efficiency, and Gissing chuckled over it.

How Gissing could stand all this "booze," to use the horrible American word, without a head the next morning, I could not un-derstand. Gissing's eyes were always clear—clearer than King Umberto's.

Curious Invitations

Despite his complaints of poverty, Gissing managed to take a social whirl during the winter of 1898 in Rome, and meet many people, more or less interesting. The invitations to dine sometimes amused Gissing immensely, and added to the joy of the many joys of that memorable season, which evidently was the happiest Giss-ing spent in his life, according to one biographer.[53]

One invitation came from an Italian Baron, and was in three languages.[54] The body was in Italian, and there was French and Eng-lish. Gissing remarked: "That man has an English wife." This proved to be true. But Gissing found in this tri-lingual invitation another supporting fact for his contention that the Italians are a bunch of delightful children.

Gissing had one complaint, I have heard from a few other people, about all this social success—it was hard on his pocket book because of the laundry of starched shirts and cab fares. Gissing's London dress suit stood up well—and sustained the reputation given [by] him to London tailors.

Gissing seldom uttered a complaint about Italian cooking—and most foreigners have to complain about the food they encounter. Gissing said once that he had lived many years on ham and eggs of cheap eating places, holes in the wall, in London, or in boarding houses at a pound a week. That is about 70 cents a day. He had lived on much less in Chicago, about seven cents a day—but we shall discuss that elsewhere.[55]

Like everyone else in Rome, Gissing ate two meals a day, luncheon and dinner, with a roll and coffee or chocolate for breakfast. He got not only food but diversion in the Italian restaurants, always preferring Fiorelli's near San Carlo at Corso in Rome because of the food, service and low cost.

Pasquale was his favorite waiter, for Pasquale had the delightful Italian waiter's manner of the past century, and a sense of humor.

One luncheon Gissing was unable to eat because of a coughing spell produced by Pasquale, who had been summoned to a table nearby to wait on an ugly, fat Englishwoman, who tried to talk Italian and who carefully studied the menu, finally ordering *petto di maiale*. This is breast of pig, said Gissing, who caught the order.

Pasquale remonstrated with the Englishwoman, declaring that there is breast of chicken and of duck, but not of pig. The woman insisted. Finally Pasquale exclaimed: "*Signora, non c'è petto di maiale. Vuole questa parte qui* (hitting his shoulder) *o questa qua* (striking his butt)." The woman, enraged, left the table. Gissing's face broke out into a rash, and he went into a fit of laughter and could not be prevailed to finish his meal. He gulped down some Chianti.

The American and English tourist in the restaurant, especially the tourist unable to speak Italian, invariably caught Gissing's fancy. The original story of the Englishwoman and the order for broiled squab probably was told by Gissing, who caught it at Fiorelli's, but it is still going the rounds in Rome, especially in church circles. This woman left the Sistine Chapel tired in the neck, after admiring Michael Angelo's frescoes, with the cracks the wily old genius had painted to prove to the Pope that frescoes would not hold on the ceiling. The woman tried to order broiled squab unsuccessfully, and then thought of the word DOVE. A dove or a pigeon would do. Unable to make the waiter understand, she got a bright idea. She had seen a dove in one of the master-pieces, hovering over Christ at the baptism. Perhaps she had seen the dove in some painting in the Vatican. So she fumbled her Baedeker for a description of that painting, remembering that Baedeker often gave the titles in Italian. But alas, when she found the *Dove* painting, the description was astounding —*Santo Spiritu,* or Holy Ghost.

Englishmen were worse off than Americans in the study of Italian, Gissing explained, because an American could make a damned fool of himself anywhere without insulting the Italians, but an Englishman's training prohibited his making *an ass* of himself. Gissing told of a prominent Londoner in Rome who was studying Italian with a woman teacher, but who complained repeatedly: "I lack practise."

"Why doesn't he try his Italian in restaurants?" I asked. That's where we worked.

"Because an English gentleman cannot make an ass of himself," replied Gissing with a twinkle in his eye.

Gissing was prejudiced.

Fair as Gissing appeared about that delicate subject of England's treatment of Ireland down the centuries, Gissing appeared to me at times to be unfair to Americans. Next to the Italians, Gissing seemed to have a feeling Americans were likely to give the most amusement in making gaiety for nations. America was a young nation filled with a lot of people who never had inhibitions, or who threw them to the winds. Or, they lacked education. Of course, it was an old saying that Americans were the tourists who made Europe laugh. American tourists were considered as a class slightly ill bred and ignorant. In art and music they showed lack of culture. The Italians, on the other hand, were superb when it came to things musical and artistic.

At the Church of San Carlo there was a big service with the robust and impressive Cardinal Rampolla officiating.[56] As the Cardinal blessed the throng with the sacred host—a wafer about three inches in diameter—enclosed in the golden receptacle called ostensorium, a woman behind me exclaimed "That's a watch he is holding up."

We Catholics believe that the Sacred Host, duly and properly consecrated, is God come upon earth, following the mandate of *the Last Supper,* to help and encourage sinful and sorrowful man. This exclamation back of me shocked. I told Gissing about it. I told him the woman was English. I so judged by her clothes and accent. Gissing replied that he had heard of the incident from an English woman he met at a tea party. He said slowly in a low voice: "She was an American woman—according to my informant." I protested that I knew she was English. But Gissing was firm. Of course it had to be an American woman who would commit such a sacrilege in a Catholic church in Rome. I could not believe that any woman would think Cardinal Rampolla would wave a watch at two thousand kneeling men and women—all profoundly devout. It struck me that Gissing was prejudiced against Americans. Gissing said the exclamation was amazing—but then—you know—these American tourists who infest Rome, et cetera.

I was so angered at Gissing I told him this story on his beloved English people. When I studied at Bruges, Belgium, our prefect of studies, Le Père Reynaert, informed me that the college had sent a dozen pupils over to England for a vacation and, as usual, several priests accompanied the youngsters to take care of their spiritual and temporal welfare.[57] As they walked through the streets of Dover, English urchins gathered around the "pilgrims" and looked intently at the feet of the priests, who wore the customary long black robes, or cassocks, and one of them yelled: "Has he got hooves like the devil?" One of the priests who spoke English asked the urchins what they meant, and the urchins, according to Le Père Reynaert, replied: "We were taught in schools that Catholic priests are like devils and their feet are hooves like those of horses."

Gissing stared at me for a minute and then broke into a violent laugh.

I was so angry at Gissing I would not dine with him the next day at Fiorelli's. But in the evening he came to see me at my rooming house—a modest private residence less than a block from his own, and bordering on *the Forum.* Gissing wished to make up, and began telling me that in England there were strange ideas concerning *the Vatican,* and would I mind listening to them? I had been instructed in my early youth by my father, a lawyer (one time chief justice of Arizona, U. S. A.), always to look at the side of one's opponent and study his arguments, and then prepare my own. I told Gissing if he wished to be fair-minded to the Vatican and to Pope Leo I would listen to him. He said that in England an impression had been given out that all was not sanctity in the Vatican; that there was more drinking of wines and champagne than fasting on bread and water. He said that a marvelous picture of the Vatican had been painted "in high intellectual circles in London," and it was as follows:

Ballet dancers roamed the long and spacious corridors of the

Vatican, and champagne corks often popped from bottles held in their beautifully carved hands. Also that these women were sparsely clad, showing a delicately chiselled hip or breast—now and then. He said that the impression was given that "high life" existed in and around the Vatican.

I told Gissing I had been in the Vatican repeatedly and I knew this was another of those "devils' hooves" lies. Gissing giggled and said: "Some day we shall see."

Gissing said that he had set foot in the Vatican Library (I supposed he had spent 1,000 hours studying in it), but that he had never been in the secret chambers. He seemed to think the Vatican and its 1,100 rooms was like some pyramid with mysterious recesses unknown to the outside world, known to a few "learned."

I determined to correct this impression by getting Gissing into the Vatican, all through the Vatican and face to face with Pope Leo XIII. Besides, Leo was a great Latin scholar, and a priest in Innsbruck told me that Leo wrote verses quite as good as those of Horace. Gissing loved Latin and Latin scholars. I felt quite sure in my boyish ardor that a face-to-face meeting with Leo would bowl over this sneering English writer.

When I mentioned Leo writing verses like Gissing's pet author, the Divine Horse, Gissing smiled that polite smile of the ironical Englishman.

At the same time, for some unknown reason, Gissing seemed to consider me a Latin scholar, for he suddenly asked me: "Can you tell me whether the Romans of Caesar's time ever wore *drawers?*"[58]

For a moment I was balked, but quickly recovering my Irish ingenuity, I replied: "Suppose you ask Lanciani, who is excavating today in your divine *Forum?*"[59]

Gissing looked crestfallen, and did not ask me any more impertinent questions during the remainder of our sojourn in Rome.

Seeing the Pope

Getting a ticket for myself to attend a Mass of Pope Leo proved an arduous task, but to get one for Gissing seemed out of the question. Why, because he was a Protestant. It seemed to be the rule in Rome to keep Protestants out of the Pope's Mass in the Sistine Chapel, or even in St Peter's.

Now, the great function which every tourist, and not a few European celebrities, wished to attend in Rome in that day was a Mass by Leo XIII. With the hordes of visitors to Rome every day, it was naturally difficult to crash the Sistine Chapel, which held only a few. St Peter's seemed easier, as 60,000 could be packed like cigarettes in a box in that largest of churches and cathedrals.

And then began a grand tour of monsignori and cardinals, of princes and powers, to get two tickets—one for Mr. Dunne, Catholic, and one for Gissing, Protestant.

Gissing marvelled at my industry and courage, but he listened with ardor each night to the recital of the day's adventures, and then regaled me with choice views of everything under the sun. It was always his effort to repay me.

It is as cheap for two to dine—when the woman does the cooking—but it was almost out of the question to get two tickets for a Leo mass.

First I tried a Prince living in a charming villa out of Rome. I had strong letters from a friend of the German *Kaiser.* The letter was in French. The prince was taking a siesta when I called, and his valet refused to deliver the missive. So we left it at the villa at Frascati. The next morning before sun-up the Prince sent two servants to ferry his reply to my apartment, telling me in beautiful French he was sorry but it seemed impossible because "*on ne donne pas les audiences.*" And there was a long sentence beginning with "*J'ai travaillé fort*" to get a ticket for one of my relatives. Gissing read the letter and chuckled: "We do not ask an audience. We can stand up at the mass."

So I worked another fortnight, and I got my Belgian princes in their lovely chateaux in the north of France to pull some wires. They had a cousin, a Palace Chamberlain, Prince, now monsignor Prince—we shall call him Croyesci—who would see me.[60] I called on the prelate-prince, going through gorgeous rooms to get to his palatial quarters in or near the Vatican. He read the letters and chuckled. Then he lambasted the Italian princes for not getting me a ticket. He said: "Just like those Italian princes to throw the work on somebody else." Then he laughed. Yes, he would get one ticket. Of course, a ticket for Mr. Gissing, a Protestant, was another matter. The rule was: Is the person a practical Catholic? A Catholic who does not go to the sacraments once a year could not get a ticket.

I had one ticket promised, and I felt sure that it would go. This monsignor prince was of German extraction—all these Croyesci family have branches in every country—or nearly every country—of Europe. Germans often are rude and blunt, but if they tell you they will get you a ticket, they mean it. If they are not going to get you a ticket, they tell you. It is said of Germans: they may call each other liars, but there is no duel over that trifling matter.

So to get another ticket I had to write to Canada, to a famous nun, who would pull wires with no less a personage than another papal chamberlain, a Monsignor, Cardinal Merry Del Val, who had been apostolic delegate to Canada.[61]

Gissing chuckled as the letters were written, and as the reply came back—very promptly—for this nun had taught me my alphabet.

And so for Gissing's sake, to get the second ticket—I finally met Merry del Val. And after all, I had nothing to do but study Italian in Rome, and I might as well see the interiors of Roman palaces. With all due credit for the lovely homes in Long Island NY, the castles or schlosser of Germany, and the Versailles masterpiece, those Palaces were something to fill the eye and brain. There was not so much comfort suggestion as pure luxury. One tourist estimated the value of brocade silk as worth $100 a foot—and it was everywhere.

Cardinal Merry del Val was a middle-aged Spaniard who was rising rapidly in Pope Leo's favor. If he ever had aspirations to the papacy—and all men are human—the one mistake he made, according to one of my friends, was in letting himself be made secretary of state. These next-to-the-pope people always "get out under" when the Sacred College meets to select—invariably a dark horse.

Merry del Val, with a strong letter from Canada, received me in a most friendly, almost fatherly manner, and proceeded to give me some good advice. "My son," he said, "this request for a private audience with Pope Leo is ridiculous. It is out of the question. All kinds of people come to Rome with extravagant claims."

In my youthful ignorance I protested to Merry del Val that an audience with the pope was not considered out of the question by important people in America, as my father was the leading worker in all the Americas for the restoration of temporal power to the popes.[62] Merry del Val stared and said he would send a ticket to the mass in the Sistine Chapel. It was the best he could do at the moment. "I have to go to a meeting now," he said and "let's walk together."

As we left the Vatican I was pleased to see the soldiers salute Merry del Val, but I grabbed a part of the honor.

"Let's take a cab," said the prelate. I waved to one of those drowsy, half drunken cabbies, who brought a cab beside us. Just as Merry del Val started to get in, he gazed at a big sign on a church plump up beside the St Peter Plaza fountains, and stumbled. I seized his arm. I thought he had a heart attack. He regained his composure in a moment and exclaimed: "See that sign." I looked at it. It was in huge letters like a pickle ad, and read "Lecture on the Immaculate Conception."

"That is at a Methodist church," said Merry del Val. "I wonder what the Methodists know about the Immaculate Conception."

"Oh, I suppose they are doing that to attract attention," I muttered.

Merry del Val asked to pay for the taxi, but I, poor as a churchmouse, refused. I wanted him to think me grand. "I suppose you went without supper 'to do that,'" muttered Gissing in a frenzy when I told him about the visit. But he chuckled at the ardor of the Methodists and the discomfiture of Merry del Val.

Two Tickets at last

At last the two tickets arrived, one from the Monsignor prince for me, and one from Merry del Val for me, but I was to give it to Gissing.

Leo XIII finally mustered up enough strength at his great age—he was nearing ninety—to say his mass.[63] And at last I would have a prejudiced English writer see the Vatican without the ballet dancers prancing around to the music of popping champagne corks.

The Mass was at 6 A.M. in the Sistine Chapel, and about 300 were invited, and I had two invites. And Gissing, his face glowing with delight—for he long had wished to see a Pope—was going. "I'll be ready at 5.30," he said, "and I'll wear the dress suit with the white tie. The invitation so ordered."

And when I called for him on the third floor of that dingy apartment house, Gissing stood there a marvelous sight in a perfectly fitting London dress suit, white vest, white shirt, white tie and all—even a watch chain, a thin chain which he insisted was correct to wear on a dress vest. Some authorities held otherwise, but he was obdurate.

And as he prepared to leave, his face broke out in a cold sweat, his hand trembled, and with drooping eyes he murmured: "I can't go, old fellow. This is awful, but I am ill. It is the phthisis that has attacked me." He begged me to leave, not to miss the Mass. Perhaps some other time, he said.

"Don't you feel you should see Pope Leo?" I asked in amazement.

"Well," said Gissing: "I *would* like to see the old duffer. But I am ill."

Down below, in the street, was a carriage with a German baroness in it. She said she had two extra seats. I had met her in my boarding house. She had heard about Gissing. When I emerged from his rooming house—alone—she asked, "Where is that crazy English writer?" "He is desperately ill with some strange disease called phthisis," I replied.

"God rest his soul," she said. "Drive on."[64]

Notes

[1] This odd phrase is put within quotation marks in the revised version, MS-B, and also in the first article, MS-C, as if Dunne got it from one of the Gissing critics he quotes there. It seems more likely that it was an oral judgment, perhaps from his friend Senator Cutting, or from one of the many literary people who visited Santa Fe.

[2] Particularly towards the final years of his life Gissing received letters from a good number of such correspondents, but their names are not easily found in the indices to either the *Collected Letters* or the Diary because the letters themselves have perished, and Gissing often refers to them indirectly. We offer a few examples, such as Miss E. T. Scott, Rosalind Travers and her family, Mrs. Henry Norman, H. H. Sturmer, and W. R. Macdonell. Among the letters of condolence, we cite that of Louise Kenny, whose devotion to Gissing was extraordinary.

[3] Gissing's blush and his extreme discomfort are quite understandable. Sixteen years earlier, Gissing had discussed the Irish question in every one of

the quarterly London Letters which Turgenev had asked him to write for *Vyestnik Evropy*, and in the first sentence of the first installment he made it clear where he stood: "Those Englishmen who have not become saturated to the marrow of their bones with party politics cannot, without burning shame, think of the mutual relations established between England and Ireland, especially about the desperate efforts of the latter during the last half century to make known its sufferings" (Jan. 5/17, 1881). The English, he said, have seldom recognized that the Irish are engaged in "a struggle which has already existed for hundreds of years," and are now at last "in a position to campaign actively for relief from the long and unfair suffering of their homeland." The fervently Irish Dunne was annoyed that "English superiority was always in Gissing's mind," but on the Irish question Gissing could not defend his own countrymen.

⁴ For Cardinal Parocchi's sermon see note 21 to MS-D. Dunne means that the subject came up in connection with this sermon, but the sermon itself deals entirely with England, not with England's treatment of Ireland.

⁵ Gissing's address was Via delle Belle Arti, 18. The owners of the *pension* were Enrico and Carlotta Gabbrielli, and it was he who died while Gissing was staying there, as recorded in the diary entry of October 17, 1897. He was fifty-one years old. Carlotta moved from Siena to Florence in 1920.

⁶ When Brian Ború's father, Edmund Dunne, set up the "Catholic Colony of San Antonio," Florida, in 1881, one of his desires was to serve the needs of the Catholic population of the area, half of whom, by the mid-1880s, were German and felt the need of a German-speaking Catholic priest. Edmund himself spoke French, Italian, and Spanish, but since his German was a little weak, it seems clear that he had sent his son to Europe to prepare him for work in this colonial project. Brian seems to have regarded the travel as preparation for journalism, a career he did engage in when he returned, but by 1902 he was helping his father to establish a German-speaking colony named Hochheim, near Castleberry, Alabama. Unfortunately, Edmund suffered a paralyzing stroke in 1903 and died in 1904, when Brian seems to have begun his many years of wandering throughout the country in search of health, as described in his book *Cured! The 70 Adventures of a Dyspeptic* (John C. Winston Co., Philadelphia, 1914).

⁷ The letter itself has not survived, but Simon Peter Cahensly (1836–1923) was a young businessman in Le Havre who became concerned with the people emigrating from that port. He was a German Catholic, part of the social movement connected with the nineteenth-century renewal of the Church, and he worked to establish in about 1871 the St. Raphael's Association, an organization which was concerned with the spiritual as well as

the physical needs of emigrants not only on the ships but also in the harbors of destination. It was therefore organized internationally, and Cahensly's efforts resulted in the German Empire's Law on Emigration of 1897. His efforts extended to securing the religious observances of the emigrants abroad, if possible in their native language, and for a time what was called "Cahenslyism" was opposed and mistrusted in America. He was also instrumental in founding missions for seamen and for Italian laborers in Germany, and worked on behalf of emigrants as a City Councillor and as a representative to the Prussian Chamber of Deputies (1885–1915) and to the Reichstag (1896–1903).

[8] Gissing's devotion to the poems of Horace is attested to by references to the poet in every volume of the *Collected Letters,* from the time in 1878 when he promised to give his brother Algernon "notes on Horace" to help prepare for an examination, to the final years in France, where Gabrielle tells us that Gissing's Sunday reading invariably included either Homer, Shakespeare, or Horace.

[9] One of the great tragedies in Gissing's life, of course, was that he felt compelled to live a covert existence ever since the scandal that led to his dismissal from Owens College and his exile to America, and which in Victorian times branded him as a criminal for life. Fear of exposure was doubtless stronger in his earlier years, but he was never anxious to reveal this episode socially, and then the perpetual problems of his domestic life thereafter prevented him from establishing a home to which he could invite his friends, other writers, publishers, or indeed anyone in the literary business, and he was always embarrassed at not being able to return their social favors. At any rate, it is clear that he never discussed any of these matters with Dunne, as can be seen in the final entry in Dunne's list of topics: "Never talked of '*my wife.*'" This may have a bearing on Dunne's subsequent description of Gissing as a "literary slave" bound by a contract, which he mentions later in this memoir and stresses in others, even suggesting that Gissing received dunning letters from his publisher. Gissing was depressed by letters from Eliza Orme bearing the sad news of his wife and child, and it seems likely that he let Dunne assume that these were depressing letters from his publisher.

[10] Several times in his letters Gissing says that he must finish the book by Christmas, 1897. The agreement with Blackie, dated September 6, is now in the Yale library, and it stipulates that the manuscript was to be sent in on December 31 at the latest. In fact Gissing finished it on November 5, but during the time he spent writing it in Siena (Dunne was with him from September 29 to October 21) there is no evidence in either the diary or the letters that Blackie was hounding him in the way Dunne describes. Perhaps both Gissing and Dunne were exaggerating somewhat, but Gissing's complaint is the kind

more likely to be expressed verbally, especially if he was trying to impress his young friend. We should also remember, however, that Gissing wanted to visit Calabria before the end of the year, so that he had to finish the book several weeks before the publishers' deadline, and that stressing the inflexible schedule was perhaps also a way of keeping people like Dunne at a distance during his working hours. On December 31 Gissing was pleasantly surprised that Blackie had set the publication date for February 15, a process he hastened to expedite because on publication he was to receive £30 on account of royalties.

[11] Dunne (perhaps with some help from Gissing) makes it appear that Gissing churned out his book with machine-like precision, exactly one page (a thousand words) a day with no corrections or afterthoughts. In fact, the diary does not quite bear this out. Gissing made a beginning of the first chapter on September 28, wrote a page and a half on September 30, and then from October 1 to November 5 wrote nearly two pages a day. He did not work on Sundays, however, and occasionally took off a day or two for some special occasion such as the celebration of fellow boarder Cappelli's final day in military service, or the death of his landlady's husband. Twice (October 16 and 30) he wrote only one page, and on November 5 it took him only a page and a half to finish the book. The manuscript does show some minor alterations, and on October 22 he rewrote one page from the previous day. According to the diary account, he wrote fifty-nine pages. Doubtless Dunne wrote of what he saw and heard, but the manuscript reveals that Gissing did make minor alterations and sometimes rewrote a page.

[12] Dickens was a lifelong influence on Gissing, who had loved Forster's *Life of Dickens* ever since he got a copy during his Lindow Grove years, when he called it "glorious."

[13] In the first volume of Forster's *Life of Charles Dickens,* chapter 6, Dickens describes the American habit of spitting out of the windows of a railway car, and then makes a general statement: "But this spitting is universal. In the courts of law, the judge has his spittoon on the bench, the counsel have theirs, the witness has his, the prisoner his, and the crier his. The jury are accommodated at the rate of three men to a spittoon (or spit-box as they call it here); and the spectators in the gallery are provided for, as so many men who in the course of nature expectorate without cessation. There are spit-boxes in every steamboat, bar-room, public dining-room, house or office, and place of general resort, no matter what it be. In the hospitals, the students are requested, by placard, to use the boxes provided for them, and not to spit upon the stairs. I have twice seen gentlemen, at evening parties in New York, turn aside when they were not engaged in conversation, and spit upon the drawing-

room carpet. And in every bar-room and hotel passage the stone floor looks as if it were paved with open oysters—from the quantity of this kind of deposit which tessellates it all over. . . ." In *American Notes,* Dickens's most trenchant comments on that subject occur in his description of the Senate, which he described as a "dignified and decorous body," and then added: "Both houses are handsomely carpeted; but the state to which these carpets are reduced by the universal disregard of the spittoon with which every honourable member is accommodated, and the extraordinary improvements on the pattern which are squirted and dabbled upon in every direction, do not admit of being described. I will merely observe, that I strongly recommend all strangers not to look at the floor; and if they happen to drop anything, though it be their purse, not to pick it up with an ungloved hand on any account. . . . I was surprised to observe that even steady old chewers of great experience, are not always good marksmen, which has rather inclined me to doubt that general proficiency with the rifle, of which we have heard so much in England. Several gentlemen called upon me who, in the course of conversation, frequently missed the spittoon at five paces; and one (but he was certainly short-sighted) mistook the closed sash for the open window, at three. On another occasion, when I dined out, and was sitting with two ladies and some gentlemen round a fire before dinner, one of the company fell short of the fire-place, six distinct times. I am disposed to think, however, that this was occasioned by his not aiming at that object; as there was a white marble hearth before the fender, which was more convenient, and may have suited his purpose better."

[14] Dickens toured America in 1842, and then again from 1867 to 1868, and it is this second tour to which Gissing refers. The weather conditions in America at the time were quite severe, and Dickens did contract a catarrh towards the end of the tour, but he himself did not connect his illness with the American adventure, and Forster points out that on his return to England his doctors were astounded at how well he looked. From that time on, however, the decline in his health was rapid, aggravated it seems by the strenuous readings he continued to give. As to the venality Dunne implies in saying that Dickens did it "for money and more money," Forster says that "No man could care essentially less for mere money," but that "the necessary provisions for many sons was a constant anxiety."

[15] The Italian novelist cannot be identified, but a number of novelists such as Katherine Anne Porter did start at the end of the novel and then go back to write from the beginning. Gissing's response here is borne out by Gabrielle in her recollections of Gissing (see the *Collected Letters,* Vol. 9).

[16] For the Croÿs, a very old and distinguished aristocratic family, see

note 60 below. Dunne's school friends at Bruges were Princes Léopold (1877–1965) and Réginald (1878–1961), sons of Alfred de Croÿ and of Elizabeth Parnall, an Anglo-Irish woman, the daughter of Charles Samuel Parnall. Their sister Marie, Princess de Croÿ, born in London in 1875, was cited for heroic conduct during World War I, setting up an espionage network for the allies, working as a partner with Edith Cavell, the famous English nurse who was executed by the Germans for helping Allied soldiers escape. Marie herself was captured and condemned to ten years at hard labor, and at the end of the war all the municipalities in the Canton of Bavay demanded that she be given formal citation by the army. She was also made *Chevalier de la Légion d'Honneur avec Croix de guerre, Chevalier de l'Ordre de Léopold de Belgique,* and an Officer of the Order of the British Empire, O.B.E. She lived until 1968, and according to Brian Boru II she was the godmother of his sister Katherine. When Dunne took his vacation with the Croÿs, they were living in the Château de Wargnies-le-Petit near Valenciennes, in northern France, but their normal residence was the Château de Bellignies, just a few miles away on the French side of the border with Belgium.

[17] Laws of international copyright developed slowly during the nineteenth century. In Great Britain there was very little such law until 1844, when the International Copyright Act conferred on foreign authors the same rights in Great Britain as those for British authors, provided the books be registered within a year of publication abroad and that other countries would guarantee reciprocal protection to British authors, a matter of separate legislation between individual countries. In America, copyright was granted only to citizen "residents," meaning persons domiciled in the country with the intention of taking up permanent residence. Even arrangements between authors and publishers for "authorized" editions were easily undermined by the publication of unauthorized editions, so that authors in neither country could gain profits by publication in the other.

The inequity of such a situation was long recognized, and during his first tour in America of 1842–43 Dickens discussed the issue quite often and even signed a petition for a copyright act, backed by the most powerful American writers and publishers, which was submitted to Congress in 1843. But it and ten others in succession were killed in committee until the first copyright act of 1891. Dickens was not the only writer to be enraged by this state of affairs.

[18] Here Dunne says that Gissing "mentioned" this point, but in his first article (MS-C) he says that Gissing "developed" it. See note 8 for MS-C.

[19] H. G. Wells noticed this too, only he thought of it not as Gissing's characteristic attitude, but one which possessed him on first seeing the

Wellses later in Paris: "The sight of us stirred him to an unwonted Anglomania, a stomachic nostalgia . . ." (*Experiment in Autobiography*, chapter 8, section 3). Here again it seems to us that Gissing was showing off to his young and naive American friend. It is true that Gissing respected and admired the culture around him, chiefly that of the higher classes, among whom he himself aspired to be counted, but it must be remembered that he was also one of the most severe critics of that culture, as his books, his letters, and his diary testify. Gissing saw the weaknesses of all nations, and England was no exception. We offer the following observation taken from his *Commonplace Book*: "The best English men & women are the most delightful of human kind. All *save* the best are endurable only to their intimates." It is fair to add that Gissing often found the common people in other countries superior to those in England. On December 9, 1897, after passing "an hour or two at Caffè" in Catanzaro, he wrote the following observation in his diary: "Tone of conversation much better than in corresponding English company. (Of course extreme temperance in drink.) Real *talk,* though never deep; clear reasoning on surface of simple and innocent subjects. Frequent recurrence of such phrases as *ingenio [ingegno] simpatico* (attractive mind) and *bella intelligenza* (beautiful intelligence). These people pay homage to intellect; is it not better (if a pretence) than the English pretence of homage to morality?"

[20] It is worth mentioning here that, during his year's residence, America was rather good to Gissing, who identified sympathetically with his new country, writing to his brother William, for instance, that the trains have "only one class, & that very much better than 1st. class in England," and "Each car is very much larger than yours in England." He had a job as a teacher in Waltham, where he was honored as an English scholar, and made a good number of influential friends in Boston. Certainly he endured the hardships of a writer's life, but in Chicago he was published by many of the leading papers, and on the whole was treated better there than he was later in London, where for a time he depended wholly on the largess of Frederic Harrison. Twenty years later it would be natural for him to remember the hardships more keenly, but doubtless his negative attitude towards America was also part of the humorous game he was playing with Dunne, who responded with acerbic observations on the customs of the English.

[21] Dunne was with Gissing in Siena from September 29 to October 21, and then in Rome from December 16 to April 12, altogether a little more than five months.

[22] Red tape was the ribbon used in securing legal and official documents, which were commonly covered with blue paper (blue-books). The term came to have a negative connotation, defined in the *OED* as "Excessive formality or

attention to routine; rigid or mechanical adherence to rules and regulations," and it was not a peculiarly American usage. The earliest citations in the *OED* are Bulwer-Lytton's "The men of more dazzling genius began to sneer at the red-tape minister as a mere official manager of details" (1838) and Carlyle's "Keep your red-tape clerks, your influentialities, your important businesses" (in *Heroes,* 1841, but dated from the lectures of 1840). This meaning had become standard usage, however, doubtless encouraged by the countless parliamentary investigations of the "Condition of England" question early in the century, when facts and statistics were gathered into blue-books and tied in bundles, so that without an adequate filing system one had to "go through a lot of red tape" to find specific reports.

[23] The "brother Englishman" was John Wood Shortridge (born in 1852 in Barnsley, Yorkshire), and the "luscious Italian maiden" was his future wife. Gissing had met him on November 20, 1888, in a restaurant near Pompeii, and spent several days walking with him, visiting his home near Sorrento, where he lived with his wife, Carmela Esposito (b. 1855 at Massa Lubrense), his children, and his brother Herbert. He was a nephew of Dr. William Wood, the Gissings' physician at Wakefield, and Gissing retained a friendship with him.

[24] The *OED* traces this word to the Turkish *bosh,* meaning empty, worthless. It became current in English from the frequent occurrence in James Morier's novel *Ayesha, the Maid of Kars* (1834), which was extremely popular, especially in the "Standard Novels" edition of 1846.

[25] Gissing finished the book on November 5, 1897, went to Rome on the 8th, to Naples two days later, and on his return stopped at Monte Cassino on December 14, spent the night there, and arrived back in Rome on December 15, Dunne joining him in searching for a room on the following day.

[26] Actually, the research was for *Veranilda,* Gissing's historical novel. It was the trip to Calabria which he took to get materials for *By the Ionian Sea,* and on his return he wrote Clara Collet: "Well, I have rich material for a little (quite a little) book."

[27] Fiorelli's was at Via delle Colonnette 4, just west of the Corso Umberto Primo and north of San Carlo al Corso.

[28] This took place on December 25, and although he complained of it, he also recognized the spirit of generosity in it: "At 12, took dinner (by invitation) with my landlord and landlady. Obliged to eat a great deal too much of very badly cooked food, followed by several glasses of Marsala. Good vulgar folk" (diary).

[29] In 1919 Dunne was city editor of the *New Mexican,* the influential

newspaper in Santa Fe, of which his friend Senator Cutting held the controlling interest. According to Richard Lowitt, in his recent biography of Senator Cutting (*Bronson M. Cutting: Progressive Politician,* 1992), Dunne had grown exhausted as a journalist, and wrote to Cutting that he had acquired business interests in Tahiti and would leave in the following January. This appears to be about the time when the American novelist James Norman Hall, author of *Mutiny on the Bounty,* took up residence there. In collaboration with Charles Bernard Nordhoff, Hall wrote a number of extremely popular short stories, and apparently Dunne also studied the short story with the two celebrated authors. The description of the conduct of Japanese men on trains suggests that Dunne had also visited Japan.

[30] Gissing first mentions Cappelli in his diary entry of October 16, 1897: "Our fellow-boarder, Cappelli, to-day finishes his year's military service. Appears in civil clothes. A good and nice fellow. O'Dunne and I bought a bottle of Marsala, to fête him with." On October 24 he mentions a talk with Cappelli ("He speaks of the increasing power of clericalism"), but does not mention him in the entry of November 1, where he speaks of the brigands: "News in paper to-day of three well-known brigands, shot dead by carabinieri, near Grosseto. They were the dread of the Maremma." The story was carried in the Roman newspaper *La Tribuna* on November 1, 1897, p. 2. Since Dunne had left Siena for Rome on October 21, and Gissing received a letter from him on the date of the newspaper story, it seems likely that a clipping from Dunne was his source of information. And since neither Gissing nor *La Tribuna* mentions Dante in connection with the brigands, perhaps Gissing had simply played a joke on Cappelli, and told Dunne the results of it either in a reply to his letter or in conversation when they met in Rome on November 8. He would then have told Dunne that "The young man went a trifle far."

[31] Marmaduke Ruggles is the narrator in *Ruggles of Red Gap* (1915), a novel by the American fiction writer Harry Leon Wilson (1867–1939), editor of *Puck* from 1896 to 1902, and author of other books such as *Zig-Zag Tales* (1896), *Bunker Bean* (1912), and *Two Black Sheep* (1931). The plot is interesting as revealing an important aspect of Dunne's frame of mind. Ruggles is the snobbish valet to "The Honourable George," younger brother and probable successor to the Earl of Brinstead. At a poker game in Paris, Ruggles is put up as a bet by the Honourable George, and lost to the American Senator Floud, whose family hopes to improve its social standing by "making something" of cousin Egbert, a diffident rancher known at home as "Sourdough." Good servant that he is, Ruggles accepts the charge of turning Egbert into a sophisticated pseudo-English gentleman, and as the family passes through New York ("the crude new American city") to the Flouds' hometown

of Red Gap, in Washington State, he struggles to adjust to his crude American employers and to a country that is proud of the equality of its citizens. In Red Gap, however, he is mistakenly reported as being a Colonel, a title which allows him to mingle with the best families, and with the help of the Honourable George's cast-off clothes and similarly discarded monocle he becomes a social lion, frequently expressing English superiority by the line "It would never do with us," which is his trademark. Touched by the American desire of making money, he opens an elegant restaurant, which becomes a fashionable business open, in the American style, to all classes of people. At Ruggles's invitation, the Honourable George now comes to Red Gap, where he is attracted to a former Alaskan dancer named Klondike Kate, and fearing that this common woman may even succeed in becoming a countess, Ruggles sends for the Earl of Brinstead to rescue George from such corruption, only to find that the Earl himself falls in love with her, marries her, and thus provides the happy community with its own local countess, an example of social equality. Now free of class pretension, Ruggles seeks out and marries a young widow, who cleans houses, tends gardens, puts up preserves, and knows how to make a good cup of tea. Having once been mocked in an amateur theatrical when a character (played by a lower-class English immigrant baker) says "That sort of thing would never do with us," Ruggles now reads the Declaration of Independence, and finding that America has made him the equal of any man regardless of birth, he becomes a staunch believer in Democracy. At the end, he is asked to read the Declaration of Independence aloud at a Fourth of July celebration, and when his wife reports that the English suffragettes are resorting to burning churches and slashing pictures, he says "That sort of thing would never do with us"—only this time America, not England, is his model. The story is a spoof on English social arrogance, and Dunne appears to have been delightfully reminded of Gissing in the person of this mere English valet, who begins as a xenophobe totally certain that England and its customs and its clothes and its classes and its food (boiled mutton) are the absolute perfection of human existence, but finally yields to the American ideal of equality. The story was made into a wretchedly distorted film in 1935 starring Charles Laughton and ZaSu Pitts, but Dunne seems to have the novel in mind, since the exact phrase "This would not do with us" (without the "sir") is in the novel as a leitmotif, but not in the film.

[32] Gissing's pension was at 41 A Via del Boschetto, which crosses the Via Panisperna.

[33] In the case of such "indelicate" words as "pregnant," it was common for upper-class Italians to substitute the French *enceinte* for the Italian *incinta*. Dunne seems to have heard the word in French, but Gissing contradicted him.

Drawing of George
Gissing by William
Rothenstein, 1897.

Portrait of Gissing by
Elliott & Fry, 1895
(Pétremand).

Gissing reading a book, taken by Mendelssohn,
1895 (University of Illinois).

Gissing in Trient,
Switzerland, August
1899 (Pétremand).

George Gissing by Elliott & Fry, May 1901 (Coustillas).

George Gissing in a
carriage window, taken
by Harold Frederic,
1896 (from *George Whale,
1849–1925*, 1926).

George Gissing, Ernest Hornung, Conan Doyle, and H. G. Wells in Rome, 1898 (from *George Gissing and H. G. Wells*).

The Pont des Augustins in Bruges, Belgium, where Dunne attended the Collège des Princes (B. B. Dunne II).

Wargnies-le-Petit, where Dunne spent a vacation in 1897 with two princes of the de Croÿ family (Photothèque Boutique-Grard, Musée de Douai).

The Château de Bellignies, near Valenciennes in northern France, where Princess Marie de Croÿ lived in the early twentieth century (B. B. Dunne II).

Brian Ború Dunne in a portrait by Datus E. Myers, a Santa Fe artist (B. B. Dunne II).

Brian Ború Dunne in a wicker chair on his porch, perhaps writing one of his memoirs (B. B. Dunne II).

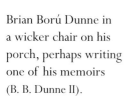

18 Via delle Belle Arti, Siena, where Dunne and Gissing were boarders (Coustillas, 1965).

A panoramic view of Siena from the Cathedral (Coustillas).

The Via del Boschetto in Rome, where Gissing lived in 1898, as it appears today (Badolato, 1997).

No. 3 Piazza di Spagna, Rome, where Gissing paid visits to Alfred Lambart (Coustillas, 1997).

[34] It was in 1888, and Gissing recorded this event in his diary entry for December 31: "Finally was tempted into the Ristorante Etruria, Via Calzaioli, and had a supper of cignale,—in vast discomfort, owing to the place being full of Italians in exuberant spirits, who were supping at table d'hôte. It made me feel wretched. At midnight they all began to shout and stamp and ring bells, etc.—a terrific uproar. I rushed out into the streets."

[35] "Unheard of" hours, literally, would be *ore inaudite* (or *ore incredibili*), but in Gissing's sentence *inoltrate* means extremely late. However, in the context, Gissing's interpretation seems quite valid.

[36] The Triple Alliance was formed in 1882, when Italy, angered by the establishment of a French protectorate over Tunisia, joined the Dual Alliance between Germany and Austria-Hungary formed in 1879. But this was a defensive move, and Italy was never as fully bound to it as were the other two allies. Italy had been weakened in its long struggle for unity, and Gissing must have been aware of the then current economic depression, the pangs of the growing industrialization, and the social unrest in Italy, which led to mass emigration from the impoverished southern regions.

[37] This was Dr. Ilario Tacchi (b. 1857), an assistant librarian 3rd class at the Biblioteca Angelica in Rome. See note 33 for MS-F, the "List of Topics."

[38] Gissing animadverts on this in *The Private Papers of Henry Ryecroft,* Spring 10, paragraph 4, where he calls it "a tragi-comical incident of life at the British Museum," and gives the wording as follows: "Readers are requested to bear in mind that these basins are to be used only for casual ablutions." But even he was not without guilt in this matter: "Had I not myself, more than once, been glad to use this soap and water more largely than the sense the authorities contemplated? And there were poor fellows working under the great dome whose need, in this respect, was greater than mine. I laughed heartily at the notice, but it meant so much."

[39] Dunne seems to have been reading Sir Walter Scott's *Life of Napoleon Buonaparte* at about the time he was writing these diaries, as we can see from "Article Two" printed below (MS-D). "Courting a cannon ball" is not in Scott, but it appears to be a paraphrase from a passage in Jacques Bainville's *Napoléon,* which was published in English translation by Hamish Miles in 1933, the year in which Dunne was encouraged by A. R. Orage to write an article on Gissing: "One has the impression that during this campaign [the Battle of Germany] Napoleon frequently courted death, or at least that he showed himself careless of death, as it would have been a way out for him. . . ."

[40] Umberto I (1844–1900), King of Italy from 1878 to his death, was indeed a popular monarch, honored for his valor as a young soldier and, as

King, for his scrupulous observance of constitutional principles, his personal concern for his people, and his extraordinary generosity, all of which earned him the name of "Umberto the Good." His popularity was enhanced by his firmness toward the Vatican, declaring Rome a permanent possession of Italy, and increased at his escape from an attempt on his life in 1897. But he was assassinated by the anarchist Bresci in 1900.

[41] Gissing arrived in Rome on December 15, 1897, and became acquainted with the Lambarts (friends of Justin McCarthy's daughter) and Swinton-Hunter (friend of Sturmer), any of whom might have spread the news of Gissing's residence in Rome. But the kind of invitation Dunne mentions did not come until the following March, and then the diary records a Miss Scott (a one-time writer for *Blackwood's*), Mrs. Charles Smith (a friend of Swinton-Hunter), Lady Edmund Fitzmaurice, and Mrs. Williams, sister of Beatrice Potter (Mrs. Sidney Webb).

[42] This was probably the Roman correspondent for the *Morning Post,* whom Gissing met at dinner with the Alfred Lambarts on December 26. His name was Frank Hurd, and Gissing described him in unflattering terms: "Detestable type; effeminate in speech; boyish in manner; age cannot be more than 25, I think. He hardly knows any Italian—is taking lessons. What a correspondent for a London paper!"

[43] Arthur Henry Bullen (1857–1920) was a specialist in Elizabethan literature, edited the works of Thomas Campion and others, started a publishing house with H. W. Lawrence, and in 1904 founded the Shakespeare Head Press in Stratford-on-Avon. Gissing records his first meeting with Bullen in the diary entry of November 6, 1891, when he was setting up the firm of Lawrence & Bullen. Gissing was favorably impressed with him from the start, and maintained a cordial relationship during the years when Bullen was publishing his books, beginning with *Denzil Quarrier* in 1892, and lasting until the turn of the century, when Lawrence & Bullen was broken up and Bullen kept the copyrights, republishing some volumes for a few years after that. Of all Gissing's publishers, Bullen treated him most fairly and generously.

[44] Gissing's account of this, in the diary entry of January 12, 1898, is quite brief: "In evening to the Orpheo, with O'Dunne. Very poor. An encore of a singer being refused, the audience made a row, refused to hear the singers still on the programme, and just went away. Oddly Italian, this. English folk would never relinquish part of their money's worth in this way."

[45] Ellen Gissing commented on this in her reminiscences, Appendix C: "It is impossible to think of anyone more affected by the weather than was my brother. If all the references in his letters and diary to weather had been included, the size of the book would certainly have been greatly increased.

Want of sunshine would plunge him into a deeper gloom at once." The American edition of Gissing's letters to his family was published by Houghton Mifflin in 1927.

⁴⁶ Once again Dunne's stress on Gissing's assumption of English superiority invites explanation, although in speech Gissing may well have adopted such an attitude for the benefit of his "naive" American friend, and Dunne himself may well be engaging in comic exaggerating, as he did when describing American doctors in his book *Cured!* In the treatment of his illness, Gissing had some scathing remarks on the noted Dr. Pye-Smith, for example, and on Dr. Jane Walker, founder of the East Anglian Sanatorium. In France, he began to conceive that in this matter the French doctors were infinitely superior to the English. Dunne, of course, could know nothing about all this, and there is no reason to doubt that he was reporting his experiences accurately.

⁴⁷ This was Dr. Riccardo Sculco of Cotrone (1855–1931). According to reminiscences that were held by his son, Dr. Silvio Sculco, Gissing suggested that Riccardo should establish himself in England, but the doctor was fond of the town in which he was a councillor and had been mayor for a time, and he preferred to remain in Calabria. In his agenda for 1897 he recorded the days he visited his English patient at the Albergo Concordia, noting his progress and the fee he charged: 24 lire. In *By the Ionian Sea* Gissing wrote down his own recollections of Dr. Sculco, whom he mentions by name, in chapters IX, X, and XI, making about the hotel bill this comment, which could also have applied to his fee: "Bill more moderate, under the circumstances, no man ever discharged." See Francesco Badolato, "Meeting Dr. Sculco's Son," *Gissing Newsletter* 10, no. 3 (July 1974): 7–8. Gissing records Dr. Sculco's command to eat steak and drink Marsala in the diary entry for November 29, 1897. The doctor's final visit was on December 4, but Gissing does not mention the prohibition on food there, although he does so rather obliquely in the entry of December 2: "The doctor, an excellent fellow. Now (the joke!) is very particular about what I am to eat." See also vol. 7 of Gissing's *Collected Letters.*

⁴⁸ Since there is no record of Gissing ever being in Verona, Dunne probably meant Venice. But the episode, which is not recorded in either the diary or the letters, could have taken place in any Italian town or city which Gissing visited.

⁴⁹ As we mentioned in note 47 above, Dr. Sculco charged Gissing only 24 lire, an extremely modest sum, for tending to him at Cotrone.

⁵⁰ Dunne's intent seems to be ironic here. Hall Caine is most noted for *The Deemster* (1887), but *The Christian,* highly touted in the press, was also a popular success, and when it came out in 1897 H. G. Wells grew sarcastic in his letter to Gissing of January 22, 1898: "But speaking of the sights of Rome

—have you seen something like this about. [Pencil drawing of Caine.] If so—shoot it! It's not human. It's Hall Caine. His damned infernal . . . book—*The Christian* . . . His damned infernal (as above) book has sold over 100,000 (one hundred thousand) copies. One hundred thousand copies."

[51] In "Article Two" (MS-D) Dunne identifies this person as Mr. Lambart, who was living at 3 Piazza di Spagna.

[52] Dunne's memory seems to have conflated two of Kipling's stories. We do not know whether Gissing had read *Life's Handicap* (1891), but in the story entitled "At the End of the Passage," the character Hummil is so depressed that he commits suicide, a tragedy due to solitude and the influence of the climate. However, he is an engineer, not an English army officer. The other story is "The Disturber of Traffic," and we do know that Gissing praised it in a letter to Eduard Bertz of October 2, 1894, calling it "especially good . . . a strong effort of imagination." Here the main character, Dowse, also goes mad, but again he is a lighthouse keeper, not an army officer, and the story is set not in India but in the Eastern Archipelago. Since Dunne quotes Gissing as saying that the story is "marvelous," we suppose this is the one he meant.

[53] We do not know what "biographer" Dunne had in mind, but perhaps he used the word somewhat loosely. Frank Swinnerton, in his 1912 critical study of Gissing, made a similar comment: "It is said of Gissing that in Italy he was always seen at his best, full of quiet fun and happy allusion."

[54] Possibly Baron Lumbroso, at whose house Gissing dined on January 15, 1898: "A party; some ten people. Among them a Miss Fitzmaurice—Irish; interesting girl (a woman rather) who teaches. On the whole, not interesting evening. The Baroness agreeable, but not very refined. The men wholly uninteresting."

[55] See note 3 to MS-C.

[56] Mariano Rampolla (1843–1913) was Nuncio in Spain, Secretary to the Propaganda for affairs of the Oriental Rite, Archbishop of Heraclea, created Cardinal and appointed Secretary of State to Pope Leo XIII, both in 1887.

[57] Honoré-Arthur Reynaert was *préfet des études* in the Collège Saint-Louis, which at that time was in the Noordzandstraat, in the center of Bruges. It is the oldest Roman Catholic college in the town, nicknamed *"le collège des Princes,"* because several princes de Croÿ had been among the pupils. Reynaert worked in the college from 1885 to 1899.

[58] See note 6 to MS-D.

[59] Rodolfo Amadeo Lanciani (1846–1929) was an archeologist and professor of ancient topography at the University of Rome, author of several

books on the ancient city. On June 10, 1897, Gissing was reading his *Ancient Rome in the Light of Recent Discoveries,* which he finished three days later, and on June 16 began *Pagan and Christian Rome.*

[60] When Dunne speaks of Croyesci he means the Croÿ family, of Belgium, a very old and very titled family dating from the thirteenth century, with branches in several European countries. As noted above, Dunne knew several princes of the Belgian branch, staying with them during his vacations, and the family was known to the Dunnes in other ways, although the precise connection is obscure. The prince Dunne speaks of here was Ferdinand (1867–1958), a Belgian and a cousin of Prince Alfred, the father of the two Belgian princes Dunne mentions. He was a favorite prelate of Leo XIII, served in the Vatican from 1893 to 1899, carrying out several missions, and was made an officer of the French Legion of Honor, a rare distinction for a Catholic priest at that time of turbulence between Church and State in France as well as in Italy. After the turn of the century he became dean of the Cathedral of St. Waudru in the Belgian city of Mons, close to the Château de Roeulx, the family home, and during both world wars he was of great help to the population and saved many lives. According to a story in the *Denver Post* (October 18, 1914), the then reigning Duke de Croÿ (Charles-Rodolphe, a German) controlled the enormous wealth of the family, and because he kept the many princes on stipend, they were moved to seek their fortunes in the business world, some of them on both sides of the Atlantic. The occasion of the story was the reported death in battle of Prince Ferdinand's brother, Prince Henri (1860–1946), who was said to be a favorite of Denver society, having an interest in coal mining there. However, this war story is contradicted by both Prince Guillaume de Croÿ, a grand-nephew of Ferdinand and Henri, in reply to a letter of enquiry, and by Georges Martin's *Histoire et généalogie de la Maison de Croÿ* (1980). According to the Denver paper, the family seems to have been related in some way to that of the Earl Grey, whose name is an English corruption of Croÿ, and both bore the identical coat of arms.

[61] Rafael, Cardinal Merry del Val (1865–1930), had been apostolic delegate to Canada in 1897 and Papal Envoy at Queen Victoria's Jubilee, and was Secretary of State to Pius X from 1903 to 1914.

[62] On March 2, 1892, at a mass meeting in New York's Cooper Union celebrating the Pope's birthday, attended by some of the principal officers of the city as well as many clergy and prominent laymen, Judge Dunne gave a fiery speech in favor of the restoration of papal temporal power. It was published in *Freeman's Journal* in New York and in many Catholic journals in America and Europe. The meeting was presided over by Archbishop Corrigan of

New York, who was quoted as saying that the speech was the "clearest, ablest and most eloquent argument in favor of the Temporal Power that he had ever heard in any place, by any person on any occasion." The *New York World* reported on the Judge himself: "He showed at once the power of the orator, he breathed magnetism and his eyes fascinated the throng." He was asked to repeat the speech on several other occasions. (Information from Quigley's "Historical Memoir of the O'Dunnes," written exclusively for the family, now in the possession of Richard Christmas of St. Leo, Florida.)

[63] Pope Leo XIII, elected pontiff in 1878, was born on March 2, 1810, and so was two weeks short of eighty-eight at that time.

[64] Gissing's diary confirms the fact that he was not able to attend this mass, but of course his account is not so dramatic. On the last day of 1897 he mentions that he has a cold, and then says that Dunne came in the evening "to offer me ticket for the Pope's Mass to-morrow morning at 8—the 50th anniversary of Leo's first mass. Promised to go if I could; but we shall have to leave in carriage for S. Peter's at 6AM." The next day, however, he was too ill: "Awake all night. Dared not go to S. Peter's, so, when O'Dunne came at 6, sent him off, and went to bed again. Did not leave home to-day; cold bad." Later, however, on February 7, "with a ticket given by O'Dunne, I went to the Vatican, to the Requiem Mass, for Pio Nono, in the Capella Sistina." And again on February 13: "Yesterday, Lambart sent me tickets for the Pope's Mass at S. Peter's to-day, celebrating the completion of 20th year of his popedom."

MS-B

The Revision of MS-A

[THE FOLLOWING TYPEWRITTEN MANUSCRIPT is a good deal shorter than the memoir above, but it is so closely related to it that we conjecture it to be a slightly altered, "improved" version, designed to bring it closer to the standards of publication—in other words, something like a completed draft, or even a final draft. First of all, the physical appearance of this manuscript is much better—the typing is neater and more regular, there are no typographic errors, nothing has been added in pen or pencil, and John Forster is correctly given as the author of *The Life of Charles Dickens.* The lines between paragraphs, which can often be annoying because of their placement as well as their inutility, have here disappeared, with the consequent improvement in the continuity of the text. The events themselves, and the comments and opinions, are very nearly identical, the slight alterations in the order and often in the wording of them clearly meant to convey a firmer sense of deliberate organization. In the longer version, MS-A, the sense of haste and even carelessness in composition, obviously allowed by the anticipation of revision, provide a pleasing sense of spontaneity, and for that reason perhaps even of the kind of authenticity which is obscured by too much reflectiveness. Yet the spontaneity is a false one, having more to do with the author's frame of mind in the act of composition than with any immediacy or temporal proximity to the events. In this version, the style is given a literary quality which convinces the reader of the author's thoughtfulness and his control over memory. This sense of sureness is sometimes even enhanced by the few added phrases, which, slight as they are, can suggest more than they say. To give just one brief example, Dunne begins one paragraph in the long version above by saying that it took three days to get an invitation from Gissing "to visit him in his room at the pension and discuss literature," and then explains that, because of his own "confined" education, he knew little of it. Here, in this version, the invitation is simply to Gissing's room, not specifically to discuss literature. Then, after repeating the same humble assessment of his education, Dunne notes that, in spite of these limitations, Gissing seemed determined to steer the conversation in a literary direction: "Nevertheless, he talked to me about literature." Finally, with unerring judgment, he adds: "We talked about nothing else." Such an observation not only sets the imagination in motion, but suggests also the earnestness of their literary concerns. It is a more reflective paragraph, doubly important because in the memoir we get few other such insights into the nature of their habitual conversations, and so lends credence to some of Alfred Morang's assertions, in his radio address printed in Appendix 1, such as that Dunne had "delved into English" and other languages "with the late George Gissing." Stylistically, even the use of longer paragraphs here contributes a sense of thoughtfulness far greater than could be conveyed in a succession of tiny paragraphs of one or two sentences each. Unfortunately, at the end of this version, in writing of the terrible Turk in the café, he thoroughly breaks up one of the only long paragraphs in the first version—doubtless an instance of the triumph of the journalistic instinct over the literary one. For all these reasons, we regard this version as an attempt to revise the earlier one for publication, and the fact that it takes up only the first section, the Siena part, suggests once again that Dunne abandoned the revision when he decided not to publish it. We have not repeated here the documentation for the larger version above.]

Personal Recollections of G. Gissing
By Brian Ború Dunne

I am writing these reminiscences of George Gissing, "perhaps a great literary man," principally for the instruction and amusement of young writers and for the diversion of Gissing's "fans" the world over. Many of them, particularly those admirers from the English-speaking countries and France, have written to him because they have found expressed in Gissing's own life the satisfaction of some inner need or desire. For in Gissing's struggles and sufferings, and, above all, in that remarkable courage shown by him, there is certain comfort for those youths, students and writers who begin again to live the life of Gissing.

I first met Gissing at a boarding house in Siena, Italy. He was tall, wore his long brown-reddish hair combed straight back, had clear blue eyes and a pale complexion. At forty (when I knew him) he was full of "pep" and loaded with ambition. When contradicted —or when some unpleasant remembrance was brought to him by a direct question—he blushed like a school girl. In my 35 years of reporting I never saw man or woman blush more violently than Gissing. I was 19 and an ardent Irishman, & I asked him: "What is the matter with Ireland? Why in the world has that country been held back? What has Ireland done to England to receive such treatment?"

He replied, "There is something wrong, terribly wrong about it." And he appeared nearly suffocated. I vowed never to return to the subject in his presence. But it came up later on—through a sermon by Cardinal Parocchi in Rome, every word of which Gissing asked me to repeat to him in the presence of H. G. Wells.

At seventeen I had gone to Europe to study the German language—conversational German. I was to live in the homes of peasants. I was to acquire the dialects in order to assist my father in a Florida land project. My father had decided that the Germans were the best gardeners in the world and the most industrious (together with the French). He decided they would be the ideal race to extract dollars from the sandy soil of Florida, where they could raise oranges and strawberries, and where they could discover, in this new land of opportunity, a rare happiness. Germany was crowded, or overcrowded. A German banker named Cahensly wrote my father: "We are increasing at 800,000 a year, & must send immigrants to America."

Before knowing Gissing, I had spent five months in Belgium studying French, and a year in Germany. I had done 1500 hours in French & 3000 hours in German. I had studied English, Latin and Greek in America.

Gissing was one of those mysterious English inhabitants in a Continental *pension*. He was a mystery even to his landlady, for he never spoke, except, perhaps, during meals, and then briefly. He became interested in me when he found out that I did not join the Italian students at the *pension* in games of pool (the chief diversion in quiet, classic, lazy Siena) but, instead, studied Horace every night. Later, I learned that Gissing was interested only in people who had studied and starved, who liked Latin & Greek, who minded their own business by not asking personal questions. (When I grew older, I understood that the observance of at least this latter point was the rule of cultured Englishmen and American Indians.)

It took 3 days in order to get Gissing to invite me to his room at the *pension*. Frankly, I had never heard of him, or of Kipling for that matter. In the year 1897 my education was very much confined to high school studies, travel and a few Continental languages. Nevertheless he talked to me about literature. We talked about nothing else.

Immediately I discovered I had met a literary slave—one who endured much in the same way as a galley slave with an "awful view ahead."

Gissing's work day began at nine, & he worked steadily through the morning. At noon, when he would emerge from his high-ceilinged room, his face would be red from the mental activity! We took an hour, Italian custom, to lunch on the delightful food of our Sienese boarding house, with a glass or two of Chianti to help digestion. And back he went to work until very late in the afternoon. Afterwards he would walk (even in this day of motor cars, Englishmen walk) and it was pleasant at those times when he invited me to join him.

In the evening Gissing would talk for an hour or two, and then retire to bed to read those books which flowed continuously through the mails.

This routine was steadfastly carried out for the six week days. Gissing never deviated from it. But Sunday was for him a day of rest. All Englishmen rest on Sundays except the bus drivers of London.

One day Gissing told me his chief trouble; he had signed a contract—and I gathered he had sealed it irrevocably by accepting a down payment—to write a volume of 80,000 words to be known as *Charles Dickens: A Critical Study*. The contract fixed a deadline at which time the work had to be completed. He received letters, I think, reminding him of that Awful Day. Such a letter, when he got it, left its mark upon his face. One could tell the day it came.

Gissing said that in writing "a critical study" he could do no more than 1000 words a day—about 6000 words a week. How he struggled!

Method of Work

Gissing would do all of his day's writing, generally more than 1000 words, on a single sheet of white paper. He wrote with a pen. As far as I could ascertain, not once did he strike out a word or change a comma!

One morning when I saw Gissing at work I delivered a letter to him—I was amazed by the discovery that Gissing traveled without a dictionary of the English language. He had a dress suit. He had a rubber bath tub. (Siena boarding houses had no tubs, and Englishmen do not go without a daily bath.) But he had no dictionary, the "bible" of every newspaper office, that book which is the hands and legs of every writer—there was no sign of it, it was non-existent.

The only book he used to assist in that splendid work on Dickens was Forster's life, a massive volume bound in green cloth.

Gissing, of course, knew a lot about Dickens before he started to read Forster's life. No doubt he had read every available book. Each night Gissing exclaimed, "This is a terrible thing—this contract!" And he assumed the air of a convict.

One day I made an injudicious reference to Forster's life, into which I peeked at times when the day's battle was over. We had been speaking of America. I remarked that Forster had published a letter of Dickens' which referred to the American travelers' habit of spitting on the marble floors of hotel lobbies. Gissing quickly said, "I have read that and for two years I have tried to forget it." It was disgusting, and perhaps unnecessary, but Dickens had that terrible gift of seeing and picturing what he saw. And the question of the materials he used and the materials to be discarded is an endlessly prolonged one.

During his study of Dickens, Gissing invariably would boil with indignation. His main and perhaps only grievance against the author of Pickwick was the American tour. "If he had stayed at home & avoided that tiresome lecture tour, he would be living today." I gathered that Dickens had some asthmatic trouble, and yet he persisted in lecturing—for money and more money.

Once in an Italian newspaper we found a success story of a novelist who had written his book in six weeks. The Italian worked ten hours a day and lived entirely on fruit. This successful writer explained, "I write my last chapters, & then go toward the beginning & see what I have to do."

All of which prompted Gissing to speak—and as for the novel, he could do many more words than 1000 in an 8 hour day. "I do not work that way. I know exactly what I'm going to do before hand. I have all the characters before me, & I proceed from the first chapter on to the end of the novel."

I had spent a vacation with some Belgian classmates (young princes) at their chateau in Northern France. Their mother was of English & Irish blood. Their sister, who achieved fame in the World

War, used to tease me about America and Americans because of what Dickens said (his inability to obtain copyrights on sales of his works in America, etc.). As everyone knows, Dickens did not spare the weaknesses of Americans.

I remonstrated with Gissing, declaring that Dickens had failed to be just in his portraiture of Americans. "But that period was years ago," he replied, and for all the world he made me feel that that generation was nearly barbaric. He was fascinated by the Belgian princess's declaration that Dickens' *Pickwick Papers* was coarse. "All women think Dickens coarse," he said with something of a sneer. I think he mentions this point in his Critical Study.

The more Gissing entered into his work on Dickens, the more apparent it became that the idea of English Superiority was in the forefront of his mind. Every nation came forward as a poor second to Great England. Gissing had traveled over all of Europe, had read of every country in the world, had met innumerable foreigners. Behind his remark lay a wealth of information, details & insights. In spite of overwhelming judgments, he was almost convincing. Literary recluse (as he has been called), he had looked upon a lot of the world.

In the evening, Gissing discussed the weaknesses of the various nations & peoples. He made a good many sarcasms about the French, and the Germans, and Greeks, and the Italians. No nation in the world amused him so much as the Italian. After all, they are quite different from the cold, diffident, supremely efficient English. And Gissing said sarcastic things about the Americans too, for he had lived in the U.S.A.

In his conversation, covering nearly a period of a year, I never heard Gissing use:

A "damn"

A "hell"

An immodest word, for that matter.

His vocabulary was so rich & magnificent that he did not require the strength to be borrowed from the reservoir of slang.

Once, and once only, Gissing found it necessary to employ

language not familiar to the rhetoric of Shakespeare & Dickens. He was remarking upon some tomfoolery of the Italian officials. "They are using," he said, "what you in America call *Red Tape*."

Once Gissing narrated what he considered a "terrible story." A brother Englishman had been "trapped" on the Island of Capri by a luscious Italian maiden. "In plain language," he began, with the air of a physician discussing some unpleasant malady, "he seduced that girl & had to marry her." Gissing thought it improper to use the word "seduce."

Gissing loved to lecture on words lifted from foreign tongues. Once he lectured me on the word *Bosh,* which, he said, came from the Turkish or Persian (I forget).

In English a common word and an exclamation of power, he explained that the word was extremely offensive to the Turk. This talk led to an unpleasant accident—in fact, almost to a murder.

One night, after Gissing had completed his splendid work on Charles Dickens, we found ourselves in Rome (Roma Immortalis). At that time Gissing was preparing for his "By the Ionian Sea." After dining at Fiorelli's on the Corso, we followed the Italian custom of sipping a demi-tasse (rather vile) in an Italian cafe so brilliantly lit up it made my head spin. All went well; Gissing drank his coffee enthusiastically and discussed with gusto the glories of the time of Caesar. And then a "terrible looking Turk" entered the cafe. He carried Oriental rugs, so bright and colorful that the effect together with the brilliance of the lit-up cafe nearly blinded me.

Suddenly I was overcome with an urgent desire to speak Turkish—and I remembered the one word: *Bosh.* I was quite young. I was curious. I wished to see whether Gissing really had the "low down" on the power of that word to enrage Turks. So I looked at the rugs for a while, and then I exclaimed: "Bosh!"

Gissing became livid. I can still hear him muttering something about "getting out of here."

Meanwhile the Turk glared, menaced—unmistakably there was a dagger-pulling gesture. The proprietor of the cafe, more than sensing danger, came rushing up. The Turk's stare intensified in proportion as his figure receded.

Gissing's coffee was spilling from the marble topped table down to the floor. He beckoned me to leave the cafe with him. With a look, more of horror than of rage, he asked, "Why did you do that?"

"I wished to see how it sounded in a Turk's ears," I replied innocently. "I never knew before how to enrage a Turk. You taught me in Siena."

Gissing walked to his rooming house, where I left him. He walked in silence. It was evident I had displeased him.

MS-C

The First Article

[THIS ARTICLE AND the next are clearly related, the second
serving as a sequel to the first, but for reasons given in the headnote
to MS-D, that one should perhaps be given a later date. Yet the first
one itself cannot be firmly dated. In the upper left corner Dunne
provides his address: "Submitted by / Brian Boru Dunne / P.O. Box
1042 / Santa Fe, New Mexico." He labels the MS in the upper right
corner: "First North American / Magazine Rights. / Ten Pages. /
2700 words." Because this article is the only one formally desig-
nated in this way as ready for publication, it is tempting to speculate that it was written in about 1935, when Dunne telegraphed
H. G. Wells that he was going to write an article for the London
Times (see introduction). But since one of the critical comments
quoted on the first page is from a book published in 1948, we seem
obliged to assign it a later date, perhaps even from the time when
Dunne was known to be writing up memoirs of famous people he
had met. The fact that he quotes from so many Gissing critics suggests that this time Dunne appears to have thought it necessary to
bring himself up to date on the current critical views on Gissing,
doubtless availing himself of the "endless library assistance" he mentions in the text. Normally, this kind of "scholarship" might be taken
as an unfortunate sign that his recollections had been conditioned
by his reading, but in comparing this manuscript with the others we
can see that for the most part his use of sources was quite restricted.

Dunne wrote about the Gissing he knew, and when he spoke of the Gissing he read about, the difference is clear. Furthermore, since criticism is a different order of writing from recollections, the quotations seem oddly inconsequential, and the fact that they contribute so little substance to his account suggests that they were simply superimposed on a manuscript he had written earlier. There are numerous verbal variations, however, and at times it seems as though his critical reading may have led him to present a more "objective" account by leaving his own personality out of the picture as much as possible. The very lively question as to England's treatment of Ireland, for example, which to Dunne was a matter of personal importance, is here presented merely as a dispassionate fact. Sometimes he tries to achieve the impersonal effect by using the passive construction, even at the cost of the grammar. For example, when he begins a paragraph by saying "In writing these reminiscences of Gissing," and then continues with "the work is undertaken," he has left the participle in the notorious dangling position, presumably to avoid mentioning that other fact—that it is he who is doing the undertaking. The curious effect of all this is that, while Dunne often uses the same phrases as in the earlier manuscripts, he sometimes surrounds them with sentences that convey a changed attitude. The substance, of course, is unchanged: it little matters whether Gissing spoke of Dickens with a "far-away look," or that he would "murmur sadly." These may seem to be journalistic clichés, but a case can be made that they nonetheless reflect more accurately Dunne's response to Gissing at the time. Again, the substance is the same: it is the tone which is altered, and occasionally some carefully observed details. Although the overall organization is also much the same, there are considerable minor rearrangements of phrases among proximate paragraphs, resulting from his taking a more reflective control over his materials. Throughout, in fact, it is this thoughtfulness which gives the article a peculiar interest. When we hear, for example, that Horace (whom he refers to elsewhere as Gissing's "divine Horse") "presented the commonplace philosophy of the ordinary man," we seem to hear the voice of Gissing straight out of the page. But in this matter, as he says, the two minds were singularly drawn together. We may cringe slightly when Dunne lets the words of Harry Hansen describe "Gissing as I knew him," and yet here too Dunne may have thought he would gain an objective corroboration of his views. And it is perhaps this kind of thing which prompts Dunne to add a new observation of his own—that, because of Gissing's shyness and silence, the other boarders "singled him out for attention"—"furtive," he adds, "but marked." In this way we are led to feel that Dunne is now paying more attention to the small nuances missing in the other versions. In the long memoir, MS-A, he says "Gissing told me he was a writer." Here, "Gissing mentioned that he too was a writer. The 'too' aligned him with authors whom we had discussed." That sounds more like the real thing. But then again, on the other hand, we are here back to the journalistic bane of tiny paragraphs, which not only disturbs the continuity of narrative, but treats the reader as if he were suffering from Attention Deficit Disorder. The ironic result of all this is that, while the impersonal detachment and stylistic objectivity give us a sense of greater fullness and accuracy, yet in these matters such rigid intellectual control is often regarded as questionable, allowing a free and spontaneous reflection to be suppressed by a more refined journalistic overlay. But presumably such difficulties can be overcome with careful reading. At the time of writing, it was too late for anything free and spontaneous, but no one can doubt the liveliness of the account. In some of these manuscripts we are told that Gissing had harsh words for people of all nationalities, and we accept that as remembered fact. Here we are told that Gissing expressed his acid comments "in terms of irony in order to maintain good taste," and we are glad to accept that too as a recollected truth, but this time refreshingly more complete—we are reminded that Gissing never used profane language. Only in an occasional metaphor are we aware of the distance in Dunne's memory. When he says that Gissing told a story "with the air of a physician conducting an unpleasant clinical discussion," there is the Dunne of the medical satire *Cured!* In a way, we are privileged here to see a writer of importance groping to express an authentic recapturing of experiences he had often rehearsed in memory. For this, it is important to read all of Dunne's versions, in spite of the repetition, to get the fullest picture in his mind.]

Personal Recollections of George Gissing
By Brian Ború Dunne

My first meeting with George Gissing took place in Italy at the close of the last century, in a small *pension* in lovely Siena. At that time Gissing was about forty years of age, in the prime and full vigor of manhood, charged almost electrically with ambition to do a classic on his "pet" writer: Charles Dickens.

Gissing, considered by important critics as "one of the first exponents of *naturalism* in English fiction," was the first writer in the English language to predict World War One—and has been described by one critic as "the most significant figure in the period of transition from the Victorian to the modern novel."[1] H. G. Wells added: "He will be read for generations."[2]

A physical inventory would list Gissing as tall, with long brown-reddish hair combed back, clear blue eyes that are often—perhaps erroneously—considered "typically English." His complexion was clear, almost to paleness; but at times he blushed like a school girl when irritated, or when criticized for errors in his Italian or modern Greek. But he turned purple when asked the direct question: "Has England tried to harass Ireland for the past seven hundred years?" To that Gissing at once replied: "There is something wrong about it—something wrong."

Another subject I found dynamite with Gissing was Dickens' lecture tour throughout the United States. He would take on a faraway look, and then murmur sadly: "Dickens would be alive today if he had refused to make that tour. It brought on a fatal attack of asthma." He forgot to mention, however, the $200,000 earned from the venture.

In writing these reminiscences of Gissing, who was "possibly a great literary man," the work is undertaken principally for the amusement, instruction and encouragement of young writers everywhere. There are Gissing fans the world over. I meet them occasionally even in my own inland spot—Santa Fe; and it is evident that people throughout the English-speaking world have read Gissing, especially his *New Grub Street*. They certainly had in France, where he had a large following.

Gissing's readers of nearly a half-century ago took the trouble to write to him from far and foreign lands. They told him of the comfort and encouragement they derived from reading of his early struggles to secure a foothold on the literary ladder. They praised his remarkable courage and fortitude. And Gissing would remark, while reading some of the letters: "Yes, I earned seven cents a day writing for a Chicago newspaper. I lived on peanuts."[3]

There was one way to make Gissing forget the fatal lecture tour of his "ideal," Dickens, and that was to ask him to read Horace, who presented the commonplace philosophy of the ordinary man. Gissing's face would reflect his inner joy the moment he opened the *Odes*. Yes, Horace drew Gissing and me together, for without Horace I might never have known Gissing. He was extremely shy.

Gissing's shyness was remarkable in the volubility of a typically Latin *pension* where all the boarders talked and acted like joyous, playful children. Gissing's shyness made him a mystery even to his landlady, an attractive young Italian matron who arched her beautiful eyebrows when she referred to her only English guest—"Signor Giorgio."[4]

Yes, Gissing was the shy and silent one.

There was one reason for Gissing's shyness, and that was terrific concentration. Harry Hansen, in his introduction to *New Grub Street* (Modern Library edition 1926), aptly describes Gissing as I knew him. "George Gissing," wrote Hansen, "stands apart from all this talent, a strange, solitary figure, fashioning his sentences with meticulous precision. . . ."[5]

The author's life blood went into any book he wrote; yet Gissing felt the thing he needed badly—money. But money would not come to him as a reward for what he did. He complained that he was impractical.

"All I can do is to write a little," he once remarked with a sad smile.

Thus Gissing moved about, from day to day. He never spoke a word to anyone except at mealtimes. Naturally, they all singled him out for attention—furtive, it is true—but marked.

There followed several perfunctory interchanges between Gissing and myself. We talked about Horace, not as Horace the agriculturalist, but as Horace the poet. This led to exchanges of part-confidence, mutually proffered.

I discovered that Gissing was interested in the man who starved. He dreamed in Latin and Greek; his interests, which he revealed hesitantly, were nonetheless steady and powerful. Of study I had plenty, of starvation little that was not theoretical, but of languages I had a Strasbourg-goose stuffing. Remember, I was only nineteen.

Casually Gissing mentioned that he too was a writer. The "too" aligned him with authors whom we had discussed. I told Gissing of various American writers, which interested him; and he told me of men like young Kipling, of whom, surprisingly, I had never heard. After a few days I accepted his almost diffident invitation to visit his rooms, to discuss literature, and there I made a surprising discovery.

Gissing was in reality a literary slave. He endured with bitter stoicism a servitude as terrible as that of any Roman galley-rower, driven by lash and timed by mallet. He had signed a contract and made it onerously ironclad by accepting an advance on account, to write an eighty-thousand word critical study of Charles Dickens! And set down in the contract was the scorpion-lash of deadline: the work to be completed by a date duly given.

Culminating life's little pleasantries for Gissing, there arrived almost daily little *bonnes bouches* from the publisher reminding him of deadline day—his "day of judgment!"[6]

There was Gissing, rolling his Sisyphian load. And how he

struggled! He told me that a thousand words a day of this type of work was his absolute limit. Six thousand words a week—for, of course, no Englishman works on Sundays except London cabbies and bus-drivers.

The day's work started at nine in the morning. Gissing would concentrate on his awful task of shredding words, like oakum, for the eager publisher. At noon he emerged (or rather someone who looked like Gissing) from his high-ceilinged room—taut and reserved from these activities. For an hour we lunched on the appetizing food of our Sienese boarding house, washed down with a temperate glass of that thin Chianti. Then, after a short walk, back to work for Gissing. He worked until 6 P.M.

All Englishmen walk, even in this advanced day and age. Merely by accepting Gissing's invitation to share the ritual of pedestrianism I learned much of his routine, aspirations and literary habits. And what I learned of his methods may be of interest to eager young writers even in this day of motor cars.

One morning I made the discovery that Gissing depended for his facility on memory and imagination rather than on mechanical literary contrivances. He did not even possess an English dictionary.

I had called to deliver a letter, to find that Gissing's room had not yet been cleaned, and his possessions spread out around him—but the writer was hard at work.

He owned a dress suit, to be sure, kept carefully in case of any sudden dinner invitation; and, a folding rubber bathtub. No Englishman ever forgets his daily bath, for it is a ritual to him, not an act of cleansing. In the same way the Englishman will walk out in the blazing Indian noonday sun, trusting only to his sense of Imperial Immunity, but Gissing's rubber tub meant real insight, for there were no bathtubs in that *pension*.

Also, there was no dictionary.

Moreover, the man did his daily stint on a single sheet of paper—one thousand words each day—with never a correction, never a strike-out or erasure, or even a change of punctuation.

Craftsmanship?

In writing the *Critical Study of Charles Dickens,* Gissing had but one textbook from which to derive his source material: J. Forster's *Life of Dickens,* a massive volume bound in green and gold. Naturally the foundation had been laid earlier in his life by his study of Dickens' writings; but I wonder how the student writer today, so dependent on endless library assistance, sources of information and all the data available for the asking, would like to undertake a task such as Gissing's, similarly equipped?

"This terrible thing—the contract!" Gissing gasped every night as he left the supper table, wondering whether his strength and patience would hold out to meet the deadline.

One afternoon, when Gissing's battle with the daily thousand words was over, I mentioned something in reference to a passage from *American Notes,* in which Dickens remarks on the American habit of spitting all over the tiles and marble floors of their Southern hotels.

"Oh, yes, I've read that," snapped Gissing, "and for two years I've tried to forget it."

Again and again Gissing deplored the fact that Dickens had ever made his American tours and written *American Notes:* "If he had stayed at home and avoided that tiresome lecture tour—the second one—Dickens would be alive today," he would say.

On one occasion a newspaper told him of an Italian novelist who could write a best-seller in six weeks, working ten hours a day and living entirely on fruit. "I write my last chapters first," said this literary marvel, "and then go on to the beginning, working backwards."

To that Gissing—the thousand-word-a-day-worker—commented: "I do not work that way. . . . I know everything I am going to do, write or say, before I start a novel. I have all my characters before me: then I proceed from the first chapter right through to the end of the book."

In view of his unbelievably neat copy on the Dickens work, I can cast no doubts on that statement.

As Gissing's work on the Dickens critique continued, it became amusingly apparent that the *idée fixe* of British superiority was always in his mind. I related an anecdote of my vacation when I was staying at the ancestral home of a Belgian classmate. He would read Dickens' *American Notes* and then tease me about my being an American. He would quote from memory passages from Dickens animadverting American manners and customs.

Now, Dickens was above all a reporter; he set things down as he saw them, and in the course of his first American tour he saw much that was different and displeasing to him.

So, for that matter, did Mrs. Trollope![7]

My Belgian friend, however, affected to disregard the fact that many years had passed since Dickens first visited America.

I told Gissing of one criticism I heard of Dickens; an English woman said, "These *Pickwick Papers* are humorous but coarse." Gissing's terse rejoinder was: "I suppose all women think Dickens coarse!" In his *Critical Study of Dickens,* published later, Gissing developed this very point.[8]

To Gissing's mind, England was the Know-all, Be-all, End-all of everything good. He had traveled extensively, not only through Europe but in America. He was very well acquainted with the world and its ways, but once and for all, first, last and always, England (My England) was supreme to Gissing.

Looking back toward those Sienese days and nights, I remember vividly Gissing's caustic analysis of French, German, Greek, even Italian culture; for he spared none the acid commentary of his ideas. But he took the trouble to express them in terms of irony in order to maintain good taste.

I have never heard Gissing at any time, under whatever stress of provocation, utter a mildly profane word. He did not find it necessary to lard his superb vocabulary with such gropings for adequate expression. Indeed, the synthesis of his uttered thoughts was superb. He never used slang even in the form of accepted colloquialisms. Only once did he slip slightly, and then it was in quotes.

Speaking of some example of exasperating stupidity on the

part of Italian officialdom, Gissing said to me, "They are using what you in America call 'red tape.'" The ineffable inflection on "red tape" and the diminuendo contained in "you in America" were typically, pricelessly English.

In relating what he thought to be a rather terrible story about a fellow-Englishman entrapped on the Isle of Capri by a luscious Italian maiden, Gissing said, with the air of a physician conducting an unpleasant clinical discussion before laymen: "In plain language, he seduced the girl and had to marry her." The word "seduce" was highly improper—at least for a Gissing in conversation.

Words were a fascinating thing to Gissing. Onomatopoeia, rhythm, flow, measure and tempo of cadence, these are all reflected in many a limpid passage in his writings. I remember several delightful discussions we had in Siena on words stolen (as Gissing put it) from other tongues. Gissing maintained the word "bosh," more in vogue then than now, was a direct appropriation from either Turkish or Persian. Exactly which no longer seems to matter.

He went on to explain that the word in English has no particular meaning, being akin to "stuff," "rubbish," or similar terms of abrupt dissent, while in Turkish it has a particularly offensive connotation, the nature of which he neglected to make clear. On this lapse on Gissing's part from true precision hinges an incident that might have been productive of real tragedy, possibly even the human drama of murder.

Shortly after the completion of the Dickens work, we found ourselves in Rome, where Gissing was doing some research for his book, *By the Ionian Sea*. After dinner at Fiorelli's—the artists' restaurant on the Corso—we deferred to the Roman habit of drinking our coffee leisurely at a nearby café. We chose one small and brightly lighted. All seemed well, with Gissing—charming as only he could be—discoursing on Roman life under the twelve Caesars. I remember him sipping his coffee, which was particularly strong, with infinite enjoyment. He was rounding a sonorous period about Augustus himself when a Turk, undoubtedly from the

Orient but questionably impressive, a rather terrible looking Turk, entered carrying an enormous load of Levantine merchandise. This he proffered for sale.

Through some horrid idea-association, the words Turk and Bosh collided in my brain. Now, when the *real* Turk, his rugs and ingratiating smile fully displayed, stopped in front of us, I looked at the merchandise and uttered one word. The word was "Bosh!"

Ingratiation gave place to aroused rage on the Turk's face.

Blandly I repeated my one Turkish word: "Bosh."

Then things started happening.

Gissing, his face livid, said something about "getting out of here." The Turk reached for something in his belt which should have been a knife to accord with his expression, but intervention came opportunely in the person of the proprietor. A word from the Italian put the Turk to slow retreat, his eyes glaring undying hatred.

Gissing uttered an imperative command.

I retreated with him, looking blankly at the Turk. I remember we left in that café, in addition to the persons and things listed, Gissing's cup of steaming, aromatic coffee, the one he had enjoyed so much. He had overturned it in his agitation.

Outside, Gissing asked me, more in horror than in rage: "Why did you say that?"

"Well," I replied, "I just wanted to see how 'bosh' sounded to the ears of a carpet-carrying Turk. I never knew before how to enrage one, and that's what your description of the word meant to me—something that would arouse a Turk. . . . That's what you taught me in Siena, don't forget."

In utter silence Gissing returned to his room. When I left him, I had a vague feeling that somehow I had irritated him.

When I left Siena with Gissing to go to Rome, I saw in his face a great longing.[9] H. G. Wells was right when he described Gissing as a writer who surrounded himself with noble senators in togas, matrons such as Lucrece, and gladiators proud to die. And Horatiuses ready to leap into gulfs *pro patria*.[10]

Yes, Gissing became a Latin when we reached Rome. He rented

a room a block or two from the Forum, and he traced Cicero's steps whenever he could take time out of his research work in the marble library.

But one day Gissing forgot his agriculturalists—Horace and Vergil; he lost the memory of the nobility, the grandeur, courage and eloquence of Cicero and Caesar. And the vision of lovely Lucrece.

For, coming out of the Forum, where he had walked reverently, he exclaimed in a sudden fit of anger: "After all, those Romans were a blood-thirsty lot!"

He suddenly thought of the death combats of gladiators when a guide offered to show him the Colosseum!

The End-

Note: It appears that George Gissing held no ill will as a result of the "bosh" incident, for the late H. G. Wells writes me on August 23, 1907—ten years later: "I remember very vividly meeting you in Rome with George Gissing way back in '97, and how impressed he was by your assiduous study of Italian ways and customs, music and language. . . ."[11]

Notes

[1] The source of Dunne's quotation is Alfred C. Baugh, ed., *A Literary History of England* (New York: Appleton-Century-Crofts, 1948), p. 1490. We do not know the source of his quotation about Gissing's naturalism, although others made similar comments, such as "Unquestionably he did go to the school of naturalism" (Herbert J. Muller, in *Modern Fiction: A Study of Values,* 1937, p. 188). Baugh also comments on Gissing's prophesy of war: "No other writer of the period foresaw more clearly the catastrophe towards which the world was heading, and no other prophesied so forcefully and repeatedly the coming of 'a time of vast conflicts which will pale into insignificance the thousand wars of old'" (p. 1493). For this see also note 14 to MS-D.

[2] The actual quotation from H. G. Wells is: "Some of his books will be read for many generations" (*Experiment in Autobiography* [1934], chapter 8, section 3).

[3] Gissing published his first stories in the *Chicago Tribune,* and then in the *Daily News,* the *Evening Journal,* the *Post,* the *National Weekly,* and the *Weekly*

Alliance. The fullest account of this publishing history is in Robert L. Selig's *George Gissing: Lost Stories from America* (Lewiston, NY: Edwin Mellen Press, 1992). From Chicago, Gissing went first to New York City and then to Troy, New York, where, as Selig says, he "lived five whole days on handfuls of peanuts from venders in the street, the cheapest meal in town."

[4] See note 5 for MS-A.

[5] Without the context, Dunne's quotation is misleading. At the beginning of his Introduction, Hansen lists the "motley array of wares . . . laid before the British public in the year 1891," including Kipling's *The Light That Failed*, Barrie's *The Little Minister*, Hardy's *Tess of the D'Urbervilles*, and Conan Doyle's *The Adventures of Sherlock Holmes*. He then continues: "George Gissing stands apart from all this talent, a strange, solitary figure, fashioning his sentences with meticulous precision, despairing of anyone's recognizing the classic pattern under its crude, English cloak."

[6] This appears to be an exaggeration. See note 10 to MS-A.

[7] In 1829, Anthony Trollope's mother, herself a prolific writer, went with her husband to America, opening a small shop in Cincinnati. The shop failed, and on her return to England she wrote an unflattering account of her three years' experiences entitled *Domestic Manners of the Americans* (1832), a book which caused a good deal of resentment.

[8] Gissing begins chapter VII, "Women and Children," with the following paragraph: "With female readers Dickens was never a prime favourite. One feels very sure that they contributed little or nothing to the success of *Pickwick*. In the angelic Oliver they began, no doubt, to find matter of interest, and thence onward they might 'take to' the triumphant novelist for the pathos of his child-life and to some extent because of his note of domesticity. But on the whole it was for men that Dickens wrote. To-day the women must be very few who by deliberate choice open a volume of his works." Gissing develops the point in the pages following this paragraph, noting Dickens's "fidelity in reproducing the life he knew," a world in which women are often "unintelligent and untaught."

[9] To be exact, Dunne left Siena for Rome on October 21, 1897, and except for three days in Rome on his way to Naples, Gissing did not see him again until December 16, the day after he returned from the Calabrian journey, when the two of them tried to find a room for Gissing. Perhaps it was then Dunne saw the longing in Gissing's face, which might reflect Gissing's attitude toward the Eternal City, although we think H. G. Wells exaggerated it in the passage quoted in note 10 below.

[10] Wells speaks of Gissing's affinity for Rome in *Experiment in Autobiogra-*

phy, chapter 8, section 3: "At the back of his mind, a splendid Olympus to our Roman excursions, stood noble senators in togas, marvellous matrons like Lucrece, gladiators proud to die, Horatiuses ready to leap into gulfs *pro patria,* the finest fruit of humanity, unjudged, accepted, speaking like epitaphs and epics. . . ."

[11] Wells's letter is printed in the introduction, together with a general letter of recommendation by E. D. Shaw, managing editor of the Washington, D.C. *Times,* dated January 22, 1906, which suggests that Dunne had asked Wells to write a general letter of recommendation for a man needing a job. At this time Dunne was engaged in his eight-year journey to find health, as described later in his book *Cured!* and he seems to have worked for a number of newspapers across the country, for which he needed such portable references.

MS - D

The Second Article

[THIS SECOND ARTICLE begins with a summary of the first, but the MS is not in the same condition of readiness to submit to a publisher. Beneath the title Dunne has written an "Editor's note" to say "Mr. Dunne studied English, Latin and Modern Greek with George Gissing for a year in Rome" (It was a little more than five months: see note 21 to MS-A). There are many slight additions and corrections in brown ink, particularly on the first few pages, and there are a good many typos, corrected and uncorrected. In these respects it resembles the manuscript of the large memoir, and it also reflects his reading about Napoleon which we saw there. It is, however, an essay of the same kind as the first article, sometimes in much the same deliberate style, perhaps written just after the first draft but left unrevised. Such first drafts are hypothetical, however, and all we can say of both articles with any certainty is that they cannot be dated.

Yet, while we get here the same sense of circumspection and objectivity, the tone itself is leavened with several colloquial phrases, such as "an occasional cat's lick" or "Gissing pined for the take-off." For the first time Dunne also seems to stress Gissing's happiness in this happy time: Gissing's "blue eyes fairly bulged with unrestrained delight," and "He looked happy—all day and late into the evening." Dunne also introduces here a number of episodes not in the other versions, particularly some interesting details of the trip to Calabria, evidently drawn from his list of topics. And there are a few details which show that the friendship, which had begun with some reserve and caution, had now become sufficiently intimate for Gissing to reveal such personal trivia as the amount of his cash allowance—about "a guinea d'or" a week. Here again are those fresh, even if trivial, details, now retrieved from the mud of memory, which lend a kind of credence to his account. It is a pity, then, that he speaks of Gissing's study at Jena University, for here is the only clear case in which Dunne let his reading intrude into his recollections. It appears that Dunne had also read Sir Walter Scott's life of Napoleon, and so we must discount the section—happily, a brief one—from Jena to the introduction of Bertz's name, where we are back on track. Certainly Gissing had talked about Bertz, certainly Dunne knew he was going to visit Bertz in Germany after leaving Rome, and certainly in *Ryecroft* Gissing wrote everything that Dunne quotes. This continuation of the first article, written in a fairly similar style but with a slightly different tone, is important particularly for introducing, after the first few pages, those materials not included in any of the other versions of the memoir. There is nonetheless a good deal of repetition, and rather than repeating documentation, or introducing a cumbersome system of cross-references, we have identified with an asterisk many items which appear elsewhere, and documented the others whenever possible.]

Personal Recollections of George Gissing
Article Two

I have told in Article One of George Gissing's slavish life, his awful "eighty days," when he wrote that masterpiece of critical study of the life and works of Charles Dickens.[1] I have described his daily task writing one thousand words, under a publisher's deadline. I have shown how he endured with bitter stoicism a servitude as terrible as that of any Roman galley-rower, driven by lash and timed by mallet.

At last Gissing quit rolling his Sisyphian load. He became a free man—to work in the marble libraries of the Eternal City, to gather materials for his new book, "By the Ionian Sea." He looked happy— all day and late into the evening.

The Ionian Sea, I discovered, is a part of the Mediterranean Sea between Greece and Italy, where it forms the Gulf of Taranto. South of the Adriatic.

Why in the name of Saint Michael Gissing selected that subject was beyond my comprehension. He had spoken in Siena of a novel he intended to write about an Englishman, one of his London friends of a comfortable income, who had been snared into marrying a luscious Capri Island maiden.[2] When Gissing visited this friend in some village south of Rome, he had been shocked by the man's un-English habit of walking around the house at night *in his bare feet.* Such a violation of the conventions had shocked Gissing, who apologized to me one day for wearing a gray flannel shirt with soft collar. "They will think me a hick," he said. (Mr. Lambart had seen him in Piazza Venezia.)*

Gissing worked joyously on his searches into history, but complained bitterly to me at luncheon one day at Fiorelli's (artists') restaurant on the Corso, that the librarian had reprimanded him for reading the London Times during the study hour. Gissing admitted that in his home town, London, the library authorities had seen fit to discipline some of the student-writers for over-use of the wash room facilities—stripping to the waist for their ablutions. He chuckled as he quoted the sign that the London librarians had erected—it contained the phrase, as I remember, about the use of the wash room for "casual ablutions." (It is rumored G washed his socks in a Museum wash basin.)*

As Gissing had no dictionary—apparently never used an English dictionary in his travels—I went to the library to find out the meaning of ablution. It seemed to me that the London librarians encouraged body bathing by the definition. But, according to Gissing, the London fussy folks wished their library-users to confine themselves to a sort of Pontius Pilate hand-washing, with an occasional cat's lick over the face.

Anyway, Gissing was very angry at the Italian's reprimand over reading the London Times in the library, and mentioned it with acute sarcasm three times in three days.

Gissing pined for the take-off—a trip to Southern Italy, with stops at Monte Cassino, famous Benedictine Abbey, and at Catanzaro and Reggio.* But the Roman library held him for weeks and weeks—Gissing leaving his London Times in his rooming house near the Roman Forum.

Gissing's sojourn in Rome was enlivened by a letter from a London friend asking him to call on Mr. and Mrs. Lambart, who were wintering in Rome.[3] Gissing's research work was seriously interrupted by these visits—to a swank apartment on Piazza Venezia where the English tourist's mecca was located—*Piale's.*[4] Gissing complained to me that Mr. Lambart was a fine London gentleman "with lords as common as blackbirds among his acquaintances," but that he had the astounding habit of showing up very late of the afternoon. Gissing was left for an hour or two—he had been asked to call at 4 P.M.—alone with Mrs. Lambart, "who shocked me by discussing birth control."* And also reading a poem from an English paper written "by a man in prison" and adding: "I know who wrote that poem." Gissing said that Mrs. Lambart had the audacity to mention the name of the poet, "a name never mentioned in London polite society"—as she explained.[5]

Gissing said that Mrs. Lambart "gushed like an open faucet," even after her husband arrived, in the library of the apartment, and that Mr. Lambart simply "punctuated with frequent coughs the amazing conversation of his wife."

As for Mr. Lambart, Gissing said that he confined his discussion to a recital of his difficulties in learning the Italian language, which he was studying with a talented Italian teacher—a young woman. Gissing explained that "people that matter" in London cannot afford to study Italian as we had been doing, in and out of restaurants and shops, on street corners and at boot black stands. "An English gentleman cannot afford to make an ass of himself through publicly expressed grammatical errors," he added.*

Gissing dreaded the visits to Mrs. Lambart's salon, as he said the London lady's conversation had grown so racy that he, Gissing, also had developed Mr. Lambart's coughing fits. But Gissing was cheered up by a letter from an English lord arriving at Rome—a friend of Mr. Lambart—inviting Gissing to an evening dinner.

Gissing was as joyous as a child receiving a new toy when he showed me the letter, written in the English King's English, but sprinkled with expressions in French and Italian.

This dinner was a greater success than the Lambarts' teas, for Gissing rolled out his London dress suit, and wore his boiled shirt and stiff collar, and white tie. And felt "au courant." He seemed to find this garb an atonement for being seen in the Piazza Venezia wearing a gray soft flannel shirt and his unpressed clothes.* G wore even a watch chain on his white vest.

Gissing said the day after the dinner that he had met an English woman whom he escorted to the dinner table, and that the food was good. The highlight of the dinner, however, in Gissing's eyes, was the English lord's act in pulling a tiny gold key from his right vest pocket and opening a gilded case which contained a bottle of Napoleon brandy—very precious. The dinner guests of My Lord evidently were impressed; they realized they were getting indeed what the Americans call their "private stock."*

It appears that at the English lord's party Gissing met the Lord's secretary, a bright young man from London, who complained that he had hoped to see some of Rome's many monuments, but that his entire time was taken up entertaining the nobleman's guests and in eating and drinking. Gissing was late each day at the Library, and his Ionian Sea research was delayed or confused by long conversations with this young man whom he encountered each day in the street. The London secretary told Gissing that he had had enough of this eating and drinking, and that his health was suffering.

"And all this food and brandy is not costing him a cent?" I asked.

"He is being *paid* to eat and drink," laughed Gissing, whose blue eyes fairly bulged with unrestrained delight.

The day arrived for the trip to Southern Italy to "get local color," to pick up "atmosphere" for that Ionian Sea book—a book I felt would be unspeakably dull except to Latin and Greek scholars of the highest academic training.*

Gissing gave me an assignment in my Latin studies—to find out for him whether the Romans at the time of Christ wore drawers. The question had never occurred to me, but I was pleased to do a bit of research work to help such an ardent scholar as Gissing.

I found the *cinctus,* a sort of petticoat like the Scotch kilt, reaching from the waist to the knees, or in that direction. This apparently was worn in early times instead of the tunic, by males engaged in laborious pursuits. It appeared on a terra cotta lamp. The Thracian gladiator also wore a sort of "undies," or lower half of present-day bathing suit, by the pictures from terra cotta lamps.

With these body-enveloping togas, like the blankets on Taos Pueblo Indians, it was impossible to see from figures I studied whether the Romans or even the Greeks wore drawers. But it was evident that both sexes were in the habit of wearing two tunics, the "underwear" of Cicero's day evidently was called tunica interior or intima, [seen on] Roman bas-reliefs.[6] It was evident that the Romans removed the cumbrous and embarrassing toga when taking violent exercise or doing laborious work. It seemed to me that the tunic was rather a one-piece suit, and not like our drawers.

After settling that subject—if I did settle the problem for Gissing—I was glad to see this novelist and classicist take off in his big overcoat and carrying an enormous valise, which really taxed the "cabby" to load it into the hack . . . bound for the railway station.

Gissing used to gloat over this canary-colored leather portable trunk—explaining that only the English knew how to tan leather. Certainly there was not an Italian-made bag to compete with it.*

Gissing made a sort of dash-to-the-North pole—it seemed to me, for in a short time he was back in Rome, with fascinating stories about his trip.[7] He had encountered rough weather facing his Ionian Sea, for there were more than breezes to blow. He said that the carriage window, on one trip, had been smashed by the awful wind. But that English real woolen invincible overcoat, and the heavy English valise to which he clutched, allowed him to win the battle.

As for the visit to Monte Cassino*—it had been delightful. Despite his dislike of all religion, Gissing warmed up to the Father Abbot, in his flowing robes, and recounted with much gusto the daily greeting in Italian.

The Abbot:

"What are you writing today, Mr. Gissing?"

Gissing:

"I am working on a historical novel."

The Abbot:

"The historical novel has its mission." *(La sua missione.)*

Gissing's eyes twinkled when he mimicked the abbot's quasi-chant: *"La sua missione."*

It seems that the literary road was rougher, and Gissing developed a fever—I think it was one of those tubercular storms, for later Gissing told me he had what he termed "phthisis" and those awful night sweats—occasionally, Gissing cursed the Italian doctor who had been summoned to his bedside, because he said "that fool ordered me to eat beef steak."* Gissing refused to do so—letting nature and his experience in a high fever guide him. Then, as he was convalescent, on the road to recovery, Gissing said "that numbskull cut off all food when I needed a life line."

In these attacks of fever and night sweats Gissing said he had discovered that the Italian medico's prescriptions, advice, and health-hints were valueless. Or worse. Gissing said that all he would take was purgatives, but they must be *English*—and invariably ordered Beecham's Pills.[8] Gissing complained of the "outrageous, extortionate charges" by the Italian chemists, or whatever they were called, "just double what we pay in London."

Once and once only Gissing denounced in scathing terms an English physician, whose honesty, he explained, had been corrupted by life in tourist-gouging Italy. Gissing got a cinder in his eye in Verona, while snooping around the alleged "grave" of Romeo & Juliette.[9] And as he made his living, however humble, with his eyes glued on a sheet of paper each day, Gissing decided to go to a real physician—an English medico. Gissing admitted that the London doctor displayed real skill in extracting the torturing cinder, but added: "When I asked him what was his fee, this extortioner said in icy tones: *'A guinea d'or.'*" This was about a week's net income for Gissing, according to the financial budget he said he was following.

As to the literary results of the tour of the Ionian Sea region, Gissing seemed satisfied, but said that while prowling around "the country" his wits were nearly scared out of him by a bandit-appearing character, who hove into the offing. Just as he got ready to give up the ghost with a knife wound [like the one] which finished off Gissing's friend, Julius Caesar, the bandit-character extended his right hand and said in Italian: "Will you buy this old coin?"

Gissing bought the copper coin, explaining to me: "There was no way out."

Back in Rome Gissing said he studied Italian daily to relieve the monotony of writing his English. He said he would paste a column clipped from the daily La Tribuna on a long sheet of paper, and then translate with a pen or pencil the sentences into English. That was Monday's study. On Tuesday he would take the big sheet of paper, fold it to hide the Italian, and put back into Italian the English. Then he would compare it with the printed La Tribuna.

Gissing was very angry one day when he ran across an editorial in an Italian paper dealing with disreputable young women haunting the streets in the early evening, as well as during that Noon Day Parade (up and down the Corso on the stroke of twelve.)[10] He also deplored the use of the word *"liar,"* which he said he had found in a religious paper's editorial, attacking the anti-clericals.

All rows and fights, religious or civilian, annoyed Gissing, who said he had found out at the age of twenty years: "Opinions are like nails—the more you hammer on them, the further they go in." (*Les opinions sont comme les clous*—etc.)

Despite his love of England, his belief that the English did everything better than any other nation, Gissing was annoyed over letters I received from a South American businessman who was visiting Venice, because the word Venice brought up a picture of Lord Byron. Gissing said that Lord Byron's life in a lovely Venetian palace was unbecoming a serious writer, especially British. He said Lord Byron had been justly criticised for association with "wanton women" flitting about amidst "popping champagne corks."[11]

As for Venice, Gissing said one of the joys of his life was spending a few days in that unique and lovely city. He was on his way—I think in the early '90's—to Athens, to tour and study. "It was heavenly," he said, "to be awakened by a sea gull, pecking at the window pane."[12] Gissing expressed horror that Lord Byron, a really grand poet, had misinterpreted his mission in Venice.

Gissing also criticised King Umberto of Italy (the poor man who was shot down by a cowardly assassin a short time after Gissing and I left Italy) for "driving around in the streets of Rome, his eyes bloodshot." Gissing said: "The old boy has been out to late parties."*

Gissing expressed the warmest admiration for Queen Marguerite of Italy, as he said he had heard that the Queen "maintained the dignity of her position, and showed a wonderful command of language." The dignity of position—by requesting a lady in waiting to return to Naples. And refraining from uttering curses when the lady in waiting replied: "I am ready to leave any time, Your Majesty, now that a friend at court has *paid all my debts.*"* The wonderful command of language—by saying to a flattering courtier: "My son, the Prince of Naples, is hardly a wonderful young man, but Madame, he has his *qualities.*" (Of course the prince referred to was later King of Italy, and after the Mussolini collapse, for some time braved the insulting shouts of *"When are you going to abdicate?"*)[13]

Gissing expressed sorrow, however, for the King of Italy, "because he has to appear as the head of an army which cannot possibly keep up with the armies of Germany and Austria." Gissing added: "The spectacle of Italy in this Triple Alliance is not only a joke, it is a tragedy. It is like a child trying to walk with a *man*."*

Gissing was possibly the first important writer in the world to feel the approach of the world-shocking, convulsing, terrifying *War One*.* It was the new discoveries, the new theories, the machines, which engaged his intelligence, but wearied him and then depressed him, as he points out in "The Private Papers of Henry Ryecroft."* All this *science* frightened him. He saw it as the remorseless enemy of mankind. He saw it "darkening men's minds and hardening their hearts."[14]

Gissing had studied in Germany—at Jena University, one of the greatest institutions of learning in the western world.[15] But Jena is or was the home of the Zeiss optical works. And these works also manufactured precision instruments. Gissing may have seen into the future—the use of precision in a world conflict and yet another world war known as *Two*. And it was in Jena, in 1806, Napoleon administered a crushing defeat to the Prussian army. Undoubtedly Gissing studied the battle of October 13 (1806) in which the Prussians "advanced, retired, or moved to either flank, with the regularity of machines" (As Walter Scott points out in his life of Napoleon Buonaparte). But the machine snapped and "there was scarcely a general left to issue orders."[16]

Gissing read of the havoc wrought by *science*. Strong towns and fortified places had been the work of "exhaustive science" only to yield to Napoleon's trumpets and bombs. The flight of shells. But the fall of Prussia, due to Napoleon's superior brand of science, suited George Gissing, for he certainly developed a hatred of Prussians during his stay at Jena, or from conversations with his German philosopher friend. I think the name was Bertz. Gissing told me that he had evidence the Prussians in the 90's had trained officers "who struck soldiers on the legs when the legs were not lifted to proper height during drills." (A German general of War One who visited Santa Fe hotly denied this accusation.)

Gissing predicted all this science would bring "a time of vast conflicts," as he words it in his Private Papers of H. R. (supposed to be autobiographical). These conflicts, he predicted, would pale into insignificance "the thousand wars of old," and will "whelm all the laborious advance of mankind in blood-drenched chaos."[17]

While Gissing considered the King of Italy and the other member of the Triple Alliance, the Emperor of Austria,[18] fairly temperate men, certainly not blood-thirsty, he distrusted the German Kaiser, with his fierce up-turned (trained upward by wearing a silk bandage in sleeping hours) mustache, his dazzling uniforms, his Martian helmets, glittering swords, and that march step. But above all, those fiery speeches.[19] This rattling of the sword. This talk of toasts ending with "Der Tag." And all this preparation for a war . . . troops everywhere you walked, rode or breathed in Germany. This system of railways, spider-web fashion, to get German troops "on the scene of action" with the least possible minute of delay.

And this climax to every public meeting with the chairman, the presiding officer, calling for *"hoch der Kaiser"* and topping it off with *"und sein Reichskanzler."*

Gissing's face blazed with indignation when I read from a German war book, printed in German, making fun of the flight and plight of Napoleon the Third of France, traveling *"Dritte Classe,"* or third class carriage. "That poor man, suffering with gall stones at the time—and those Prussians making fun of him," was Gissing's comment.[20]

Gissing's hatred of the German Kaiser, because of the Emperor's war-like attitude, and for no personal reasons, reached its culmination when I showed him an Italian Sunday supplement in color, portraying the danger to His Imperial Highness. It seems Emperor William was out in a row boat in some bay or ocean, and a great passenger liner nearly ran him down. Nearly *"spurlos gesenkt"* [sunk without a trace]. After studying the picture Gissing commented: "I wonder what inspired the passenger boat's captain to change his course? Will there be an investigation?"

Gissing hated any clothes that looked like a uniform, and he severely criticised Hall Caine,* the then popular and later to be more and more popular English novelist, "for walking on the popular Corso (main avenue of Rome for tourists on foot and Italian nobility in carriages) in a golf coat and tight fitting military trousers. And worse than all—long waving hair. And a beard."

Hall Caine "sure" caused a commotion, and he had plenty of money to dine at swank restaurants. Gissing, however, hated any display on the part of an Englishman—any eccentricity of dress or carriage. As for the Italians—they could do as they liked, and Gissing chuckled and roared at their extravagances. Two in particular: (1) every Italian in a restaurant in Florence ringing bells, even pulling the silk ropes to summon waiters, on a New Year's eve,* (2) an Italian nobleman shouting to the waiter in a crowded fashionable restaurant: "Please cook the omelette in fresh butter, not oil, as my wife is pregnant."* *(Poiché la mia moglie è incinta.)* "It is never done with us," Gissing pointed out. "But here they brag about lawful pregnancy."

There was one feature of Italian life in Rome Gissing disliked —and that was these sermons by famous prelates suggesting that England should come back to Mother Catholic Church, "from which she had strayed." Gissing asked me to repeat a portion of one address, as I heard it in the fashionable San Carlo al Corso, during a May Devotion Service, where the archbishop in robes and mitre had referred repeatedly to "questa isola." And he said nice things about England's past, present and future. Gissing's comment: "Did the archiepiscopal address hold out hope of an early return?"[21]

As he toiled over Roman history, and wrote the results of his Ionian Sea ramble, Gissing suddenly discovered one day that I had moved from the region near the Forum to a tenth floor room on Via Gregoriano. And nothing would stop him from climbing up to my room, despite his rather shaky health, because he said: "You are in the exact spot, and I believe the exact room, where Gregorovius lived."

And then he told me of Ferdinand Gregorovius (I had never heard of him) who lived from 1821 to 1891, who wrote the History of Rome in the Middle Ages. And the Life of Emperor Hadrian.

German historian and poet, great authority on Italy, especially ROME.

Gissing said he recognized, from my high story window, scenes in Rome, depicted in the writing of Gregorovius.

Coming up to my rooming house one day, Gissing showed his extreme sensitivity, for he shuddered as he entered a narrow street. Pointing to the name of the street carved in white marble, he muttered: "Via degli Incurabili. What a name. The street of the incurables."

(END OF PART TWO.)

Notes

[1] Gissing wrote the book in 39 days, from September 28 to November 5.

[2] As noted above, this Englishman was John Wood Shortridge (who was not, however, a London friend), but this is the first time we hear that Gissing was planning to write a novel about him. Perhaps, however, Gissing said merely that the man's life was worth making a novel of, or he mentioned to Dunne his use of his meeting Shortridge in *The Emancipated*. In his letter to Gissing of August 11, 1903, Shortridge asks Gissing "When are you going to help me write my life? . . . What a queer jumble it would make." He is mentioned in Manuscripts A and B.

[3] The London friend was Charlotte McCarthy, daughter of the Irish historian Justin McCarthy, with both of whom Gissing corresponded occasionally. Gissing met with the Lambarts several times while in Rome in 1898.

[4] The address of Piale's reading-room was Piazza di Spagna, 1. It sold English and American newspapers at a monthly rate, and had a lending library of over 23,000 books in English, French, German, and Italian.

[5] The poet was Oscar Wilde, and the poem was "The Ballad of Reading Gaol," published by John Lane in January 1898, not in an English paper, but under the signature of "C.3.3.," which was Wilde's prison number. The authorship was not really a secret, however. It immediately went into multiple editions, and a number of critics called it one of the greatest poems in the English language.

[6] The word is *subligaculum,* which was a cloth worn round the loins, beneath the outer garments. One hopes that Dunne was being humorous in looking for an undergarment on the artifacts he mentions below.

⁷ Gissing's Calabrian tour began in Naples on November 10, and he returned to Rome on December 15.

⁸ Beecham's pills, a popular proprietary herbal digestive and laxative medicine, was invented by Thomas Beecham in 1847, and had reached an extraordinary popularity by 1887, when his son Joseph helped him to expand the business even further, advertising it with the famous slogan "Worth a Guinea a Box." Joseph, himself a man of musical taste, was the father of Sir Thomas Beecham, the distinguished conductor. (In 1924 the firm was sold to the financier Philip Hill and later began producing other patent medicines, but produced also a minor scandal in England with one of its Christmas ads: "Hark the Herald Angels Sing, / Beecham's Pills are just the thing. / Peace on earth and mercy mild, / Two for adults and one for child.")

⁹ This is confusing because the tomb alleged to be Juliette's is in Verona, but there is no evidence that Gissing had ever been there. In spite of this detail, Dunne must have mistaken Verona for Venice, where Gissing stayed in January and February 1889, and then, after returning home, set out for Greece in November. In an 1892 *Baedeker* we find a Dr. Barker listed as a practicing oculist resident from October to May. If this is the one Gissing consulted, the fact that he was a professor of medicine may account for his exorbitant charge.

¹⁰ These were the prostitutes, elsewhere referred to as *orizzontali*.

¹¹ Byron lived in Venice from November of 1816 to April of 1817, but he returned there in May, and it was during this second period that he spent the summer in the Villa Foscarini, a palace just a short distance from Venice, and then in March of 1818 the Palazzo Mocenigo on the Grand Canal. In Venice Byron led the kind of life Gissing describes, which earned him the epithet *stravagante* among Venetians, and was talked about even among gondoliers, a life which Byron himself admitted was dissolute, regretting the gossip which made its way back to England. But he also wrote a considerable number of poems there, including *Manfred, Beppo,* and the fourth canto of *Childe Harold.* It is difficult to know what Gissing means by Byron's "mission in Venice" in the following paragraph.

¹² Gissing was in Venice from January 30 to February 26, 1889. One of his first impressions was "The intense quietness of Venice. The dipping of oars below my window, and the slow moving lights of gondolas," and later on "white gulls were flying about the Canal, under my windows" (diary).

¹³ King Umberto of Italy, who reigned until his assassination in 1900, married his cousin, Margherita Teresa Giovanna (1851–1925), Princess of Savoy, in 1868, and they tried to establish a more sociable court than his father had done. She had a strong and ambitious personality, described in the

1971 *Britannica* as "the only uncontestably regal character in modern Italian history." She used her influence over her husband to make the monarchy a powerful ally in the politics of the conservative right. The son, born in Naples in 1869, married Princess Elena of Montenegro in 1896, and became Victor Emmanuel III on the death of his father, ruling as a constitutional monarch. He offered the premiership to Mussolini in 1922, and although Mussolini rendered him powerless, the king continued to support the dictator until his downfall in 1944. Victor Emmanuel abdicated in 1946, the year before his death.

[14] Gissing did not, of course, predict World War I specifically, but he comes very close to predicting an imminent conflict in chapter XIII of *The Whirlpool,* where Harvey Rolfe has been reading Kipling's *Barrack-Room Ballads* as the voice of "the strong man made articulate," a call to the men of the world to revolt "against the softness and sweetness of civilisation," a speech often misunderstood by the critics. Kipling's language, he says, is "the tongue of Whitechapel blaring lust of life in the track of English guns," but it is clear that Gissing also has Germany in mind when Rolfe speaks of improving the physique through the rise of athletics and of bicycling, two popular social trends which Bertz and other German critics were writing about as beneficial to the nation, although Bertz was critical of the idea. Rolfe speaks directly of Germany, however, when he complains that the English can't "make money quite so easily as we used to" because the "scoundrels in Germany and elsewhere have dared to learn the trick of commerce." Emperor William II's foreign policy entailed an alarmingly increased naval program which, along with his enormous military machine, enabled him to advance his vast colonial and commercial aspirations, but brought him into opposition with Britain, forcing her into the Entente Cordiale with France, and contributing greatly to the outbreak of World War I. Gissing was prescient when he has Rolfe ironically express the "reasonable hope . . . to see our boys blown into small bits by the explosive that hasn't got its name yet." In *The Private Papers of Henry Ryecroft,* Gissing touches on these matters in "Spring XIX," where he fears that the rise of "monarchic power based on militarism" (such as Germany) may see nations "tearing at each other's throats." His musings in "Summer VI" make it clear that he was convinced the European powers were headed for war, and in "Summer VII" he discusses an article he had read on international politics, in which the author not only predicts a great European war but also, in the whole tenor of his writing, "proves that he represents, and consciously, one of the forces which go to bring war about." Dunne's quotation here and a few paragraphs below, however, come from "Winter XVIII," where Gissing's topic

is not war, but science: "I hate and fear 'science' because of my conviction that for long to come, if not for ever, it will be the remorseless enemy of mankind. I see it destroying all simplicity and gentleness of life, all the beauty of the world; I see it restoring barbarism under a mask of civilization; I see it darkening men's minds and hardening their hearts; I see it bringing a time of vast conflicts, which will pale into insignificance 'the thousand wars of old,' and as likely as not, will whelm all the laborious advances of mankind in blood-drenched chaos."

[15] The rumor that Gissing studied in Jena was repeated many times until about the 1950s. It was first put into circulation in a reminiscent article in the *Nineteenth Century* (September, 1906) by Austin Harrison, who mistook as autobiographical a chapter in *Workers in the Dawn* which was actually prepared by Eduard Bertz. Unfortunately, it gained currency when it was repeated by Thomas Seccombe in the *Dictionary of National Biography,* an account which was regarded as reliable for many years. Dunne could not have got this from Gissing himself in Rome, but is clearly augmenting his recollections with what he had read since then.

[16] This was a double battle, the more important combat being at Auerstadt, but called the Battle of Jena because it was there that Napoleon was engaged in person. Scott describes the battle on October 14, not the 13th: "The battle then became general; and the Prussians showed themselves such masters of discipline, that it was long impossible to gain any advantage over men, who advanced, retired, or moved to either flank, with the regularity of machines." But Napoleon, strengthened by the troops of General Ney, soon "compelled the Prussian army to give way," and after a series of attacks, says Scott, "The rout became general. . . . All leading and following seemed now lost in this army, so lately confiding in its numbers and discipline. There was scarcely a general left to issue orders, scarcely a soldier disposed to obey them. . ." (*Life of Napoleon Buonaparte,* Volume V, Chapter 34, in *Prose Works of Sir Walter Scott,* Edinburgh, Robert Cadell, 1835).

[17] See note 14 above.

[18] This was Franz Joseph (1830–1916), Emperor of Austria and King of Hungary, who in 1867 created the dual Austro-Hungarian monarchy. He suffered territorial losses in the Italian War of 1859 and in the Austro-Prussian war of 1866, but his reign was occupied with the discontent of national minorities, and he engaged in no other wars until the annexation of Bosnia and Hercegovina in 1908. By comparison with William II of Germany, he could be regarded as a pacifist. In 1914 the assassination of the heir apparent, Franz Ferdinand, was the spark that touched off World War I. In Italy in 1898 the

powerless Umberto I was King and the government of Premier Rudini was about to fall, but his renewal of the Triple Alliance in 1891 was a defensive, not a bellicose, action.

[19] After the fall of Bismarck in 1890, William II took a more personal control of the government, and committed himself to economic and colonial expansion. He was indeed a militaristic monarch. German imperialism was a dominant theme in his speeches, and his policies contributed greatly to the events causing World War I.

[20] Napoleon III, the nephew and at the same time adopted grandson of Buonaparte, was proclaimed Emperor of the French in 1852, but by 1870 his fortunes had reached a nadir, and he was destroyed by the Franco-Prussian War in that year. He set out to join his army on July 28, but was suffering so badly from the stones in his bladder that he could hardly sit on his horse, and when he surrendered on September 2 he was taken as a prisoner to the castle of Wilhelmshöne, near Cassel, doubtless the journey on which Dunne says he was forced to go "third class"—that is, in an uncomfortable carriage like ordinary poor travellers.

[21] This was a sermon by Cardinal Lucido Parocchi (1833–1903). He took a degree in theology and canon law, was ordained in 1856, and was named Bishop of Pavia in 1871, a title he took without official sanction because of the prevailing discord between Church and State. In 1873 he had founded the periodical *La scuola cattolica,* in which he sustained austere principles bordering on religious intransigence, and he published a series of pastoral letters, homilies, and ecclesiastic discourses and lectures. He was transferred to Bologna to become Archbishop in 1877, and in the same year was created Cardinal by Pope Pius IX. In 1882 Pope Leo XIII called him to Rome, where in 1884 he became *Cardinale vicario,* remaining in that office until 1899, when he was made vice-chancellor of the Church of S. Romana, and then "segretario dell'Inquisizione" and Associate Deacon of the Sacred College. We have no record of the sermon Dunne heard, but Parocchi published in a volume of his *Discorsi* (1898) an essay or "sermon" entitled "Maria SS. regina de' profeti e il ritorno dell'Inghilterra all'unità della Chiesa" ("Most holy Mary, queen of prophets and the return of England to the unity of the faith"), in which he referred to England as a *nobile isola* and hoped for *"il ritorno di sí gloriosa nazione al centro dell'unità."* In Dunne's second article, MS-D, he says this sermon was delivered at a "May Devotional Service," but in the memoir of Senator Cutting (MS-E) he says he heard it in the winter of 1897. In the Church calendar, May is known as Mary's month, but in the later accounts, below, Dunne says he told the story in the presence of H. G. Wells, who left Rome on April 12.

Dr. Francesco Badolato of Besana Brianza suggests that Dunne meant to say "Mary Devotional Service," as suggested by the title of the sermon, and that perhaps the service was anticipatory of the month. Unless Gissing asked Dunne merely to repeat the anecdote for Wells's sake, the sermon must have been delivered between the dates of the latter's stay in Rome, March 8 to April 12. The same anecdote is told in the Cutting memoir (MS-E).

MS-E

Excerpts from "Personal Recollections of a Friend"

[DURING HIS LATER YEARS, Brian Ború Dunne spent considerable time writing up memoirs or sketches of the many important people he had known. Many of these appear in the manuscript of his massive volume entitled "They All Came to Santa Fe," which was never published. Among the longer memoirs, the most important is that of Senator Bronson Cutting, who had dropped out of Harvard because of his tubercular condition, and took up residence in Santa Fe for his health. As he said in later years, he came to die there, but instead, his improving condition allowed him to pursue an important political career at a time when the Territory of New Mexico was destined for statehood, and then to become the state's first U.S. Senator. Dunne, who eventually became the Senator's personal secretary and land agent, befriended him from the start, and with other friends attended him during his illness. When Dunne discovered that Cutting was an avid reader of Gissing's novels, he began to "regale" his friend with stories of the five months he spent with Gissing in Siena and Rome—which he counted as a year to include his correspondence with Gissing until his own recall from Rome. He recorded some of these stories in the memoir he wrote of his friend, and in order to keep his comments on Gissing together, we present those extracts here. All that need be said about them is that they do not represent a continuous memoir, and so there is no purposeful or meaningful organization. They are simply a record of the kind of stories Dunne told to his friend during the Senator's illness. But we do learn here that W. D. Howells denounced Morley Roberts's scurrilous book, that it was Dunne to whom Gissing wrote about the American divorce laws, and that Dunne was H. G. Wells's guide in Rome when Gissing was too busy. Ferrer, the typewriter salesman, does not figure in the other memoirs in this volume, perhaps because the story is only incidentally about Gissing, but the fact that the name does appear in the list of topics (MS-F) reinforces our speculation that the list was drawn up before any writing took place. Dunne says that the Cutting memoir was written for certain members of the senator's family, but the fact that he signs it "anonymous" and refers to Cutting only as "my friend" clearly means that he wanted to avoid possible action for libel, a sign perhaps that he intended it for eventual publication. In several places we have substituted Cutting's name for "my friend."]

Extracts from the Memoir Entitled "Personal Recollections of a Friend"

Bronson Cutting rarely read *Dickens,* but on two occasions borrowed from my tiny library a vellum bound copy of David Copperfield. His friend Dr. Bishop once remarked: "I cannot read Dickens—too many details."[1] My friend agreed with Morley Roberts in "The Private Life of Henry Maitland," that the charm of Dickens is a literary gem on every page.[2]

As for Gissing, Cutting apparently had read all of his novels and approved of them as literary works of art. He learned much of Gissing from me, and listened attentively night after night for weeks to stories on Gissing, his method of work, his poor pay, his struggle with poverty and with marital unhappiness. He was tremendously surprised by Morley Roberts' book, which William Dean Howells denounced as an outrageous breach of confidence— but which was written to warn other writers—no doubt.[3] My friend was particularly amused at Gissing using *me* to get him information on the divorce laws of the U.S.A. with the camouflage that he, Gissing, wished to use the material for a novel! Judge O'Dunne of Baltimore looked up some of the laws for me, to give to Gissing. It seems Gissing intended to get a divorce in the U.S.A., and then abandoned the idea. Gissing was a superlatively unhappy man.[4]

Cutting studied Gissing's career carefully, and found that the popular and polished classicist was pretty sad throughout his life, save for the period of one year when I was with him in Siena and Rome. I was only 19 years of age, and some people said I pepped up Gissing by my innocent and absurd questions and boyish enthusiasm. Gissing had smiled for two days at this dumb question I propounded to him: "Have you read Vanity Fair—a lot of it?"

My friend was amused at Gissing's sarcastic remarks [when I told him and Wells] about a sermon delivered by the late Cardinal Parocchi in Rome one night in the winter of 1897, concerning England and the history of a great island that once had been under the wing of the Catholic church—an island that should return to Mother Church. Gissing asked in the presence of H. G. Wells, with deep sarcasm which made Wells chuckle:

'Did His Eminence offer any hope of an early return?'

Cutting liked Conrad and read all of his works. He described Conrad as the writer "of the most marvelous English seen in modern times." Later my friend said there was talk that D. H. Lawrence wrote even better English.

Gissing had invited H. G. Wells to visit Rome when Gissing and I lived in Rome, the winter of 1897 [March, 1898]. Wells and Mrs. Wells came for a fortnight [actually a month], stopping at a Piazza di Spagna hotel.[5] I was Wells' guide around Rome—when Gissing was too busy to roam the streets. My friend asked me about every word Wells spoke. He would ask: "And what did Wells say?" . . . . My friend was not well impressed with the writing of Wells, until

Wells grew older. Later in life my friend said Wells's short stories were excellent. He was much disgusted with an article Wells wrote on The Balkans for that Harper's magazine with flamboyant covers then edited by Norman Hapgood.[6] He considered it silly.[7]

A short time before he died Cutting finally met Wells in Washington, and took him to luncheon in the Senate luncheon room. Wells talked freely of the importance of Huey Long. Wells looked upon Long as the coming man in America.[8]

My friend said: "Wells asked me: 'How is Mr. Dunne? Is he a man of parts?' I told Wells: 'He is.' Wells added: 'Gissing knew Dunne much better than I. But we were all together in 'Rome.'"

Cutting said that he seldom enjoyed a description of three men roaming around a city as [he did] the stories of Gissing (aged 40), English classicist; H. G. Wells, London journalist (at that time) aged 30 years, and one B. B. Dunne, American student (aged 20), walking around the Eternal City, especially prowling around the Roman Forum with George Gissing lecturing on the subject. My friend shouted in glee: "A great trio. It would be hard to beat that—Gissing, Wells & Dunne!"

Cutting was amused to violent laughter at the terrific dislike Gissing took to Luigi Ferrer, European typewriter representative for the Underwood Typewriter Company, but in 1897 [1898] in Rome representative for the Elliott & Hatch Booktypewriter Co— a machine invented to write into books to save sewing the sheets. Gissing, it was said, was *no snob,* but he denounced Ferrer as a mere typewriter salesman and thought I would get no mental uplift from running around with such people. I told my friend: "After all, Gissing was earning seven cents a day writing for Chicago newspapers some time in the nineties [the seventies], and Ferrer was drawing down ten dollars a day in gold—and I thought Ferrer a man of parts."

John Galsworthy was in Santa Fe about 1923 and heard the story at a tea party, and commented: "I might understand *Wells* being annoyed at your going around with a typewriter salesman, but not *Gissing.*"

Gissing was particularly annoyed at Ferrer for two reasons: Ferrer told risqué stories, with Latin temperament, in cafes. Ferrer had written me a letter: "I have just arrived in Venice, Italy, and the strangest sight meets my eyes—there are no taxicabs drawn by horses."

Gissing said: "Ferrer is an incredible ass." At a luncheon given for Wells, I mentioned Ferrer being bitten by a dog—on his fingers—and Ferrer asking me to learn to typewrite on the Elliott and Hatch machine to write his company in New York. "And who is *Ferrer?*" Wells asked, with his big blue eyes widening. "Ferrer is an ass," replied Gissing, as he carved a slice of an omelet to replenish the plate of Mr. H. G. Wells, who sat at his left. Mrs. Wells was there and she snickered.

Ferrer was probably or possibly an ass—he arrived in Baltimore in 1897 or 1898, looked me up, but I was out of town, called on my brother Judge O'Dunne and said to O'Dunne on short acquaintance (according to the judge): "I did well in France; I married a rich girl in Paris." Judge O'Dunne was furious. "How many typewriters have you sold in France since you took over the Underwood agency?" he asked Ferrer. "Forty," replied Ferrer. "That man is a fool," commented Judge O'Dunne to me afterwards.

Ferrer said that he had had three uncles presidents of the Republic of Columbia. A learned lawyer hearing this commented: "I do not doubt it at all. Don Pedro at the Phila Exposition saw a wheel that made so many hundreds or thousands of revolutions to the minute (as advertised on a card in front of the machine), and tartly commented, 'That beats a South American Republic.'"

Cutting was intrigued with the way Gissing visited The Forum daily and *brooded* over Julius Caesar and Cicero. "He is just like Gordon Gardiner,"[9] he said, "sticking around the Acropolis all day." My friend asked me to tell him every word that a German shopkeeper had said to me in German, while I was in Rome, when I met this shopkeeper in a park and invited him to walk through the Forum and hear from my lips the wisdom that had flowed from the lips of Gissing concerning the Forum, Caesar and Cicero. The German, a rather small man with an uninteresting face, the mouth of which held a cheap German cigar, replied in German of a rather 'peasant' accent:

"Ach was! Das ist nichts." [Bah! That's nothing.]

Gissing's comment was bitter, spirited, and a gem of satire—the bitterest outbreak perhaps I heard Gissing make in a year of conversation: "Why did you not tell that ignorant ass that a visit to the Forum would have been lost on his dull and stupid mind?"

I had planned to visit Athens when I was called home in 1898. George Gissing wished me to go to Athens, a city he had visited. My friend was extremely amused at a letter sent to me in Rome by Professor Agonosthakos, aged *ninety-eight years,* the letter in English and beginning:

> Mr. Gissing has spoken of you to me. I am a disciple of Homer and Socrates. Come to see me, my dear sir, at my hotel in Rome and I shall initiate you in the wonders of the Greek language.

Notes

[1] In June of 1910, the future Senator Bronson Cutting, whose tuberculosis had cut short his undergraduate career at Harvard, went to Santa Fe, as he said, to die. Brian Dunne had arrived there the year before, and the two became instant and lifelong friends, Dunne eventually becoming the senator's secretary and land agent. Although Cutting had met and been advised by Dr. James Massie, of the Sunmount Sanitorium, he soon took on as his medical attendant Frederic Bishop, an English doctor who had performed a similar role for his tubercular older brother, William Bayard Cutting, who had died while spending the winter in Egypt. During periods of confinement, Dunne and another friend, H. H. Dorman, tried to keep Cutting amused and interested in other people, and by the beginning of 1911 Dunne and another close friend, Miguel Otero, began to share bachelor quarters with him.

[2] Dunne evidently has in mind a passage from chapter 6 of *The Private Life of Henry Maitland:* "One finds the same thing in Dickens' writings. His page is full. It is fuller than the page of any other English writer. There are, so to speak, on any given page by any man a certain number of intellectual and emotional stimuli. Dickens' page is full of these stimuli to a most extreme degree."

³ This is an ambiguous statement. If he means the book was *written* to warn other writers of the hardships in the life of a writer, then he seriously misunderstood Roberts's intention. It seems more likely he meant that the book should be *taken* as a warning to writers that they may be dealt with posthumously by their friends in the same way Roberts was dealing with Gissing.

⁴ Although Gissing had permanently separated himself from Edith, his second wife, at the time of his departure for Italy in September of 1897, his legal marriage to her was the chief impediment to any such relationship with Gabrielle Fleury, and it was during his "courtship" of her that he began to pursue seriously the idea of a divorce, which he thought might be obtained in some other country. He had heard that Leopold von Sacher-Masoch, who had a similar problem, was able to marry his second wife in Heligoland, a story known to Gabrielle from the first wife, with whom she was friendly. On this he consulted Eduard Bertz, asking him also about the rumor that a divorce could be obtained in Hermannstadt in Hungary. He had also asked his friend Morley Roberts for information on getting a divorce in America, but when Roberts could offer no advice Gissing seems to have remembered that Dunne's brother Eugene was a lawyer and a judge on the Baltimore Supreme Court, and so he wrote asking Brian to get the information he needed. In *The Private Life of Henry Maitland,* Roberts said that Gissing wrote to a Baltimore lawyer, but this is the first time we discover that he wrote to Brian under the pretext that he needed the information for a novel. However, the passage in the memoir of Senator Cutting suggests that Brian did not discover Gissing's intention until he read Roberts's book.

⁵ The Wellses stayed at Fischer's Hôtel-Pension Alibert, in the Vicolo Alibert.

⁶ Norman Hapgood (1868–1937) was an editor, publicist, and reformer. In 1897 he assembled a notable group of writers and editors to revitalize the *New York Commercial Advertizer,* and wrote biographies of Daniel Webster (1899), Abraham Lincoln (1899), and George Washington (1901). At the same time he developed an interest in the theatrical scene, and in 1901 wrote *The Stage in America, 1897–1901.* He assumed the editorship of *Collier's Weekly* in 1902 and became editor of *Harper's Weekly* in August of 1913, staying with it for two or three years.

⁷ The article Cutting disliked was "The Liberal Fear of Russia," in the issue of September 19, 1914 (pp. 268–70), written somewhat in the tone of a man who has just paid his first visit to Russia and returned with all the answers. Such a fear, he says, will affect British and Americans during and after the war, and English Pan-Slavism will take the place of Pan-Germanism, but

only because Russia is so greatly misunderstood and overestimated. The country is too vast to be capable of unification, wrote Wells, the people are illiterate and superstitious, and a vast part of the population lives at a level "a little above that of the Aryan races in Europe before the beginning of written history." Western Europe, he says, will not have to fear Russia for two hundred years. "While Russia has the will to oppress the world, she will never have the power; when she has the power, she will cease to have the will." The Russians, "a naturally wise, humorous and impatient people, will not be reduplicating the self-conscious, drill-dulled, soulless culture of Germany." The "Krupp-cum-Kaiser dominance of the world" is more dangerous. One section which Cutting doubtless regarded as silly is a paragraph on the Balkans, which is of ironic interest to us even today: "The balance of power in the Balkans, that is to say, incessant intrigue between Austria and Russia, has arrested the civilization of Southeastern Europe for a century. Let it topple. An unchallenged Russia will be a wholesome check and no great danger for the new Greater Servia, and the new Greater Roumania, and the enlarged and restored Bulgaria this war renders possible." The article was reprinted as chapter 8 of *The War That Will End War,* 1914.

[8] Huey Pierce Long (1893–1935), a farm boy from Louisiana, became a traveling salesman, completed the Tulane University law course in seven months, served on the state railroad commission and the public service commission, and was elected governor of Louisiana in 1928, entering the U.S. Senate in 1931. He was responsible for the building of much-needed roads and hospitals and for such educational benefits as free textbooks, in these ways securing the support of the poor, but he was a clever demagogue with an enormous lust for power, notorious for corruption and extravagance, and ran his office like that of a dictator. H. G. Wells must have been impressed by Long's "Share-the-Wealth" program, which he strongly advocated in the Senate and on his lecture tours, outlined in his book *Every Man a King* (1933). He next aspired to the presidency, but was assassinated in 1935.

9. Gordon Gardiner, a dilettante friend of Cutting's brother William, was with Cutting during his stay at a sanitorium in the Swiss Alps and during his visits to archeological remains in Egypt, Greece, and Italy at the time of his undergraduate years at Harvard.

MS-F

The List of Topics

[IT IS NOT POSSIBLE to assign an exact date to any of the documents printed here, but it seems reasonable to suppose that the following list of topics was drawn up before any of the written memoirs, and served as a source from which he drew the incidents. In the absence of anything like "original" notes, written during or shortly after Dunne's months with Gissing in Italy, it would be desirable to establish the earliest possible date for this list, and it is tempting to argue that he set down his memories early in his Santa Fe period, when, during his friend Bronson Cutting's confinement for a serious illness, Dunne was regaling him with anecdotes about Gissing. But in the first and longest memoir Dunne says he is writing thirty-five years after the events, which would place the memoir in 1932 or 1933. Clearly the list itself was a preparation for the writing, and most of the episodes in the memoirs conform to the headings in it. As an aid to the reader, we have identified those episodes by introducing the following code letters at the end of each appropriate entry: A = the large memoir; B = the revision; C = the first article; D = the second article; E = the memoir of Senator Cutting. The list itself is valuable in suggesting the range of Gissing's conversations with Dunne, but since many of the topics were not used in the memoirs, we have tried whenever possible to suggest the kind of anecdotes or stories Dunne might have had in mind. A few of them, such as the account of Stella in the *Café Chan-*

tant, are known from Gissing's diary or other sources, but Dunne's version is invariably fuller and often quite different. Several others, such as the mere name of Gladstone, can be augmented by reference to Gissing's letters, and some can be explained at least partially by biographical and historical investigation. But most of Dunne's opinions, comments, and stories about Gissing are quite new, and it is regrettable that so many of them were left out of the memoirs and will remain forever unknown. They do, however, suggest a good deal about his friendship with Gissing, which was eventful enough, but also rich in conversation.]

Personal Recollections of George Gissing

Analysis:
Chapters—
His arrival in Siena; first meeting at luncheon. Greek with Cappelli. (A,B)
His appearance. (A,B,C)
His work—a writer. Book on Dickens. Its title. (A,B,C,D)
His method of work. 1,000 words a day on this critical work.
   (A,B,C,D)
His references to Forster's Life. (A,B,C)
His daily remark about Dickens—"might have been living today except for the American tour." (A,B,C) Dickens; asthma.
   (A,C)
Women's opinion of Dickens. (A,B,C)
The horror of a contract to deliver a MS on time. (A,B,C)
The typing of it 1,000 words at a shilling.
Life in Siena. (A,B,C)
People he discussed:
Kipling—book on India. (A,C)
H. G. Wells. (A,B,C,E)
Gladstone.[1]
The Royal Family. (D)

English lord who gave a guinea. (A)

The women before theater. (A,B,C)

The landlords and landladies he had known in Italy. No bath. (A,B,C)

The Italian army compared to Triple Alliance. "Child walking with a man." (A,D)

Horace and how he should be read. (A,B,C)

Greek.

The will to succeed.

The Episcopal minister.

His story of doctors. (A,D)

His story of his education.

Doctor who tried to make him eat heartily while ill; when recuperating, "Niente." Wine and beefsteak with high fever. (A,D)

Newspaper obituaries—people die and then we hear of them.

Method of learning languages.[2]

Story of visit to Athens—and the seagulls in Venice. (D) The fish in oil. The tip question. "My visit to *Grease*."[3]

Acropolis. (E)

Method of work on a novel. (I read account of Italian novelist who worked backward.) (A,B,C)

Correspondence and its cost. The morning horror.[4]

Letter from Australia.[5]

Letter from woman who would meet him in Paris.

Request for cheery message concerning a book. Illustrations good.

Letter which told how GG had had a hard time—as told by a boy in London. (A)

Clippings from newspapers cheered him.[6] Bjornson.[7]

Amusement over Italians at depots—on trains—anywhere. (A,D)

The American, too. (A,B) "Bravo" in a theater to a woman. Errors in English tickled him. The man who broke the back of Monte Carlo.[8]

Latin stories. *Obit anus, abiit onus.*[9] Dislikes *noster me oleum*.

His American experiences—Bitterness. Left Boston as he
  wished to see the world. Worked for 7 cents, in Chicago;
  lived on peanuts. (A,B,C,D)
Got red in face in discussing Ireland. (A,B,C) Something wrong
  in management of that country. (A,B)

Liddell and Scott, Liddell and Scott,
Scott did it and Liddell did not.[10]

Disgust for pictures of Italian women with full bosoms.
His walks on Sundays. (A,B,C)
Tarring of birds for sport. Outrages for poor Uccellini.[11]
Baths—dreaded to get head wet. His own bathing equipment.
  Rubber tub, carried it around. (A,C)
His story of German friend and philosopher, Bertz. (D) Clip-
  ping of *fein* [unintelligible word] *Herr.*[12]
Discussed The Whirlpool as important.[13]
Tells of visit to Naples, blood in bed. Murder of an English
  woman. She had lived 17 years in Naples.
Asks me Latin word for "drawers." (A,D)
Discusses Sarah Bernhardt.[14]
Doctor in Verona Louis d'or for a cinder. (A,D)
Weather—weather. (A)
Denounces dancing—Romans used slaves.
To use plain language—"seduced" that girl (Capri story).
  (A,B,C,D)
Talks much of Dr. Johnson and Boswell.[15]
Dislike of wrangling—discussion—controversy. (D)
The zither. Dreary music. Why it was so terrible—man dying of
  cancer.[16]
Financial matters. $ a week. (C)
Life in London. (A) Ordering of food.
Vanity Fair—all of it?[17] (E)
Napoleon III—and dritte klasse. (D)
Marion Crawford and 15,000 a year. Different thing.[18]

 END SIENA

The List of Topics 143

Boarding house.

Restaurant. (A)

The Forum. (A,C,D,E)

Cafe chantant. Greatest kick. Two francs a week. (A)

Calls for *"Stella."* Fuori la Stella. (A)

His landlord and the Christmas dinner with pound of cheap candy. (A)

Library. (A,D) His experiences in Rome and Florence. Remarks about newspaper. (A,C,D) Also about English system and baths. (A,D)

Pope Leo. (A)

The Vatican. Views in England. (A) Swiss guards operatic.

See Lambart and snobbish corres. Morning Post. Monsignori brought this man news. (A)

Restaurant at night. Sees duplicate of Bullen the publisher. (A)

Woman in restaurant who asks for *petto di maiale.* (A)

Restaurant where Empress of Austria dined.[19]

Rooming house where Gregorovius lived and Cardinal Vaughan visited.[20] (C,D)

Society. Dining out. Invitation from a Baron in 3 languages. (A,D)

The English lord and the gold decanter with mysterious key. (A,D)

Secretary who could not keep the pace. "He is paid." (D)

Italian dinners sent in tin boxes to pensions. (A)

"Aspasia" name of girl in Florence. His comments.

His love of pure English. (B,C) Never used hell once, red tape and damn. (A,B)

Enraged at Italian paper "orizontali."[21]

Disliked anti-quirinal papers for using word "Liar."[22] (C)

Discussed his publishers—not paying him enough. Their visit.[23]

They stop at Grand Hotel and ask him to call at Strand.

Lambart studies Italian with private teacher. Can't make ass of himself. (A,C,D)

Bishop Stonor and 42 years of Italian.[24]

Englishmen go to Italy to live in style—cheaper.[25]

Dislikes portrayal of English tourist in play "Io essere."

Not an English woman who said "Is that a watch." (A)

Disliked Cardinal Parocchi's suggestion *"quest' isola"* might return to church. Sarcastic in front of Wells. Any hope? (A,B,D,E)

Tells stories of Queen. (A,C,D)

King had bloodshot eyes. His remarks. "Out a bit late." (A,C,D)

Typewriter salesman raised his ire. An ass. (D,E)

Disliked German who said *"ach wass"* about Forum. Told me what to tell him. His face red with anger. (D,E)

Romans, ancient, were a bloodthirsty lot. (B,C)

The Royal family and clothes.

Italian count who yelled *"Poiché la mia moglie."* (A,C,D)

My modern Greek "Kálista." He said Ka-list´-a. It is first syllable.

Liked story of Agonosthakos.[26]

Greek teacher who was an angel. (D)

Austrian who gargled before meals.

English tea parties. We see one in action at Wells's hotel.

The woman who talked about abortions. G. coughed. And hawed. (A,D)

GG is interviewed. Man wrote with pen and ink.[27]

G's love of industry. Liked people who had starved and read Latin. (A,B,C)

Singers at night and *Basta.* 3 A.M. (A)

Keeping a diary. "Life is drawing to a close."[28]

Calls his ailment "phthisis." (A,D)

Teaches me Persian—*"Bosh."* Our experiences with a Turk. It is an insult. G angry but helpless. (A,C,B)

"Whore" a good English word. He always used prostitute. (A) Woman violinist in St. Peters.

Climate in Rome in January. Light a match in Pincio. (A)

Gossip at hotels. Old man and young wife.

Booksellers. Disliked haggling. *Je ne fixe pas le prix.*

Favored journalism as a starter.

A stable position in America.

Read my interview with Justin H. McCarthy.[29]

Wells in Rome.[30] (A,B,C,D,E)

Hall Caine in Rome. (A,D)

Story of Henry Norman and secret of success.[31]

G's love of fancy cakes. (A)

No love of sports.[32]

Disliked Castellane publicity.

Italian women get fat at 25.

Tacchi the librarian. (A,C,D) Salva tacchi.[33]

Zola.[34]

La Bohème and breaking up of furniture.[35]

Americans love exaggeration.

My story of the Czar. Danger of bombs. His remarks.

His visit in Calabria, mounted police, sale of a coin.[36] (C,D)

G never had a dictionary. (A,B,C,D) "I play."

G's dislike of a reference of Dickens to oysters.[37] (A,B,C)

Was G a prig?

He shudders as he enters street *"Via degli Incurabili."* (C,D)

G discussed how it must feel to be Pope. "Serious to be locked up for life."

Rampolla well nourished and the lean Leo.

The mass for Pius IX—black vestments.[38]

Lambart's remark about dress suit at 6 AM coming home with the milk in London.

G as a linguist.[39]

He would translate on Monday; put it back on Tuesday. (C,D)

G's stories from Bertz about Prussian military discipline and cruelty. Cane blows for failure to do Russian calisthenics. (C) This is denied by German generals. (C,D)

Dislike of German emperor.[40] (C,D)

Bertz said "You offer me food I have not sunk so low."

His love of luxury.

Visit to Monte Cassino.[41] (C,D)

Flannel shirt in Piazza di Spagna. (A,C)

His love of Music. Perkins at the piano.

His story of humorist who wished to slap a bald man (Doctor).

Contrast English and Italian nobility.

His hours in bed, studying ceilings.

Balancing a tea cup on his knee.

Italian nobleman in Rome asking alms—driving carriage.

The Pope's poor relations.

Seminarian I met climbing hills, out of breath and saying "*de promissionibus Jesus Christi*" ["Concerning the promise of Jesus Christ"].[42]

In Athens hotel upset as he asked for a bath.

Never talked of "*my wife*."

Notes

[1] William Ewart Gladstone (1809–1898) was in Italy at the beginning of 1889, when Gissing was in Florence, and Gissing was amused by the daily newspaper stories which reported Gladstone in terms of an exaggerated courtesy that seemed comic to him. In his letter to Bertz of January 20, 1889, he quotes from the *Corriere di Napoli,* which was, along with the *Secolo* of Milan, the only Italian newspaper he thought worth reading: "You have heard perhaps that old Gladstone is at Naples. Well, the *Corriere* has something about him every day, & always in a strain of delicious hyperbole. At Pompeii the other day he was offered a cup of tea, & he accepted it '*con squisitissima affabilità*'! But this is a trifling example."

[2] Gissing's interest in teaching languages is evident in his letters, from the time when he was instructing his sisters about their proposal to set up a private school in Wakefield. But he doubtless told Dunne about W. T. Stead's treatment of the subject in several issues of the *Review of Reviews* in 1892. This series of articles was occasioned by a method devised by a French scholar, François Gouin, and presented in his book *L'Art d'enseigner et d'étudier les langues,* translated into English as *The Art of Teaching and Studying Languages.* Stead experimented with the method for six months, using his own family as subjects, and reported the successful results in January of 1893, in an article

entitled "A Royal Road to Learn Languages: The Result of a Six Months' Experiment." Gissing commented on it in his letter to Algernon of February 9: "You saw Stead's experiment in the new way of teaching foreign languages seemed fairly successful. It seems to me a rational method enough. I shall never let Grobsey [his son Walter] toil for weary years over Greek & Latin grammar & exercises, with the result at the end that he cannot read a Greek or a Latin book. It must be managed differently somehow."

[3] Gissing was in Athens from November 19 to December 17, 1889. The pun on "Grease" is explained by a comment in his letter to Algernon of November 29: "A restaurant is attached to the establishment, & one eats *à la carte; very extraordinary dishes I eat, too, occasionally. Everything swims in oil.*"

[4] Gissing was always sensitive to the cost of postage, and his concern increased as his fear of poverty grew, especially during his final years in France. In 1899, for example, on June 4 he sent some autographs for the sale of some of his books, and told his sister Ellen "in any case I grudge the postage." On October 22 he noted that the Authors' Syndicate had charged 9/- for postage and delivery of MSS: "As I cannot remember a similar item in former accounts, would you kindly let me know what period this covers?" On December 22 he apologized to his agent, W. M. Colles, for having refused to accept a letter with insufficient postage: "Of late I have rather often paid excess postage on letters which contained only circulars, or something of the kind; so, when the post-man demanded *eightpence* on yours (which bore only 1^{d} stamp) I declined to pay." This was a problem on which Gissing commented in his *Commonplace Book:* "The English are the only people in the world habitually guilty of the discourtesy of sending letters abroad insufficiently stamped. It comes of their impatience of detail." In fact, this burden of having to pay the price of insufficient postage annoyed Gissing so much that he once lodged a complaint with his agent Pinker: "By the bye, your clerk occasionally understamps a letter, putting 2 ½^{d} when the weight is over ½ oz. & in this case I have 5^{d} to pay at this end—too heavy a tax in these days of cheap postage" (November 28, 1902), and finally told Colles not to trouble "about taking in letters to me from strangers; they are never worth postage" (February 15, 1903). By the "morning horror" he doubtless means waking in the morning to face the horror of the day's work ahead, as did Reardon in *New Grub Street.*

[5] This letter is explained in Gissing's diary entry for October 3, 1897: "The poor fellow, Allhusen, of Gateshead, sends pitiful letter, saying he has to go at end of October to Australia, probably for life. Wrote with what encouragement I could." Ernest Lionel Allhusen (1875–1943) went to Australia for his health, was cured there of tuberculosis, and became an avid book collector, whose collection of 400 volumes is now in the National Library of Scot-

land. Gissing's reply to Allhusen's letter, dated October 3, 1897, is printed in the *Collected Letters*, 6:353–54, and his earlier letter of July 12, dealing with book collecting, is on pp. 310–11.

⁶ He probably means clippings about *Charles Dickens: A Critical Study*. Gissing was flooded with reviews of the book supplied by Durrant's Press Cuttings, London, to which his agent Colles had subscribed on Gissing's behalf.

⁷ On Björnson, all we learn from the diary is that on October 12 and 13, 1892, Gissing bought and read his *The Heritage of the Kurts,* and that on October 12, 1894, he sent it to Algernon. In the letter to Algernon of September 17, 1892, Gissing noted the remarkable treatment of the book in Stead's *Review of Reviews*. On October 22, 1899, he sent Björnson a copy of *The Crown of Life*.

⁸ "The Man Who Broke the Bank at Monte Carlo" was the title of an extremely popular song (at that time, and well into the twentieth century), which is sung by Lou at the beginning of "Lou and Liz" ("the man that browk the benk at Monty Car-lo!"). The mistake Gissing mentions was then common enough (and even now, among those who still remember the song), so that he did not record any specific incident in either the diary or his letters.

⁹ "An old woman dies, the burden has gone away." *Noster me oleum* seems to be highly elliptical, perhaps meant only to remind Dunne of a longer phrase he wanted to use in the memoir. It does not call to mind a common Latin phrase, however, and it is in itself unintelligible, although *oleum* (oil) can mean hard work usually done at night. If Blackie's was indeed putting Gissing under the pressure of a deadline, as Dunne describes earlier, then Gissing may simply have resisted the pressure of night work, but of course we don't know whether the thing he "disliked" was the phrase itself or what it meant.

¹⁰ Henry George Liddell (1811–1898) is known chiefly as the father of the little girl who served Lewis Carroll as a model for Alice. However, together with Robert Scott (1811–1887), he compiled the famous *Greek-English Lexicon*, first published in 1843 and, in a revised form, still in use today. The *Oxford Dictionary of Quotations* gives us the following anonymous rhyme:

> Two men wrote a lexicon, Liddell and Scott;
> Some parts were clever, but some parts were not.
> Hear, all ye learned, and read me this riddle,
>   How the wrong part wrote Scott, and the right part wrote Liddell.

We do not know whether Gissing was quoting another popular version or was making up his own shortened version of it. But Gissing's version reverses the meaning, since Liddell is known to have worked more on the lexicon than Scott, and certainly longer, publishing a revised edition in the year of his death.

[11] In the diary entry of October 20, 1897, Gissing does speak of *la caccia,* the rather cruel luring of small birds, such as thrushes and finches, using blinded birds as a decoy enticing the others to branches smeared with lime: "When the birds alight there, their wings get limed, they fall down, and a man rushes out to kill them with a stick. Moreover they are caught in folding nets, worked by a string, and beaten dead or their necks wrung. . . . They eat all the birds thus obtained." "Uccellini" is a diminutive meaning "little birds."

[12] Eduard Bertz must have been a particular topic of conversation with Dunne because Gissing was to make his only visit to his German friend on April 12, 1898. In fact, his quotation, later in this list, of Bertz's words "You offer me food I have not sunk so low" suggests that the conversations were quite vivid, but unfortunately the only other hint of them in these memoirs is the treatment of the Prussian officers in "Article Two" (MS-D).

[13] Gissing regarded *Sleeping Fires* and *The Paying Guest* as somewhat minor novellas, and so in effect *The Whirlpool* was his latest novel of substance written for the better sort of reader. In it he discussed parental responsibility and the education of children quite earnestly, and in his eyes the book was also significant as an expression of his anti-imperialism and his pacifism.

[14] Gissing saw Bernhardt in *Frou-Frou* at the Gaiety in London, in June of 1882, and again in March of 1886, during his first visit to Paris, he saw her in Sardou's *Fédora.*

[15] Gissing first read Boswell sometime before November 13, 1876, when he agreed with his brother Algernon that it was amusing. In a letter to Madge of November 27, 1880, he provided the following assessment: "Old Sam Johnson was in many respects an admirable man. He was a terrible Tory, of course; but I can forgive him much in consideration of the *genuineness* of his character. When he said a thing, he meant it; & I believe his life was in accordance with his beliefs. Now & then he was a little too fond of argument for argument's sake, but then he liked to exercise his intellect on different sides of questions, & I daresay he did not dislike to come off victor. There can be no doubt that he was a good-hearted old bear, as the records of his home life testify." To Ellen on January 31, 1885, he said "The book makes an epoch in one's life." For an excellent treatment of the subject, see David Grylls, "The Annual Return to Old Grub Street: What Samuel Johnson Meant to Gissing," *Gissing Newsletter* 20, no. 1 (January 1984), 1–27.

[16] During this Roman stay Dunne sat for a photographic portrait, which appears as an illustration in this volume, showing his zither on a table beside him. In his letter to H. G. Wells of June 15, 1912, he identified himself as Gissing's friend "who played (?) the zither for your benefit, with Gissing remarking 'You're out of practice my boy.'" The dying man was the husband of

Gissing's landlady in Siena, mentioned in the diary entry of October 14, 1897: "For a year and more the husband of Signora Gabbrielli has been lying paralyzed, dying." The man died three days later.

[17] At the age of nineteen, and without any specifically literary training, it seems likely that Dunne had trouble following the intricacies of this very long Thackeray novel, and part of his youthful naiveté was to assume that others did too. But doubtless he was humorously referring to its great length.

[18] Francis Marion Crawford (1854–1909) was a novelist and historian who was born of American parentage in Bagni di Lucca, Italy, where his father was a sculptor, and who lived most of his life in Sorrento. His first novel, *Mr. Isaacs* (1882), was an immediate success and determined his career as a prolific writer, turning out sometimes two or three novels in a single season, and writing more than forty of them in twenty-five years. The "15,000 a year" may refer to the sales of his books, but is more likely a speculation about his income. He was indeed immensely successful, but as Neal R. Shipley notes in "'The Constant Question of Finances': The Ordeal of F. Marion Crawford" (*University of Mississippi Studies in English* n.s. 6 [1988]), he spent his income even before he earned it, and his whole life was a constant pursuit of money. Outwardly he lived in high estate in his famous literary home in Sorrento, Villa Crawford, attended by a retinue of devoted servants, and as Shipley points out he appeared to be "first and foremost a gentleman" and "a cosmopolitan aristocrat." Yet he was forced to write compulsively at every moment of his life, eventually churning out novels which he himself admitted were potboilers. When Gissing says "Different thing," however, he doubtless means different from popular writers such as Hall Caine, who also earned a fortune with his own potboilers. But Crawford was a highly educated man who studied in at least three Western countries, and knew not only most Western languages but also Russian, Turkish, and nearly all the Eastern languages, spending more than a year in the East studying Sanskrit. Some of Crawford's works are not without merit, but although Gissing did not much like the seven novels he read, he must have respected this highly cultured and adventurous man, much as did Henry James, who, as Shipley says, "despised Crawford's novels but was at the same time deeply impressed by their author." When Gissing made the comment recorded by Dunne, he had already asked Henry Norman (see note 31 below) for a letter of introduction to Crawford, whom he hoped to meet at Sorrento on his way to Calabria in order to get letters of introduction to useful people there. In Naples on November 15 he had still not received the letter, but at that time Crawford was making money on an elaborate, two-year speaking tour in America, where, as Shipley notes, he wrote constantly, "writing on pads held on his knees in

trains and snatching odd minutes under gas lights while waiting for connections."

[19] This was Elizabeth of Bavaria (1837–1898), wife of Franz Joseph I, Emperor of Austria (1848) and King of Hungary (1867), an Empress highly revered in Hungary, not only for her generosity and philanthropy, but also because she insisted that the coronation of her husband to the dual Austro-Hungarian crown take place in Hungary. She was thus instrumental in the reconciliation of Austria and Hungary, but was assassinated in Geneva in 1898 by Luigi Luccheni, an Italian anarchist, who wanted to "cause all those arrogant people who fill such positions to fear and tremble."

[20] Herbert Alfred, Cardinal Vaughan (1832–1903), succeeded Cardinal Manning as Archbishop of Westminster and was responsible for the building of Westminster Cathedral.

[21] *Orizzontali,* "the horizontals," is a jocular Italian reference to prostitutes.

[22] The Quirinal Palace has been the residence of the monarch or the president of Italy. During the struggle over the Papal possession of land, the anti-quirinal papers were Vatican papers criticizing the royalist government.

[23] Gissing probably told Dunne of the occasion in November of 1891 when Arthur Henry Bullen came to Exeter, inviting Gissing to dinner at his hotel. The visit must have been indelibly impressed on Gissing's memory, since Bullen then treated him more generously than any other publisher had ever done: "Altogether unlike a publisher; no business reserve; 'I want to give you as much as ever I can, consistently with some profit to ourselves'" (Letter to Algernon, November 6, 1891). But he undoubtedly remembered also an earlier time, when no less a personage than George Smith called on him to invite him to dinner (Letter to Margaret, June 13, 1886).

[24] Edmund Stonor (1831–1912) was Archbishop of Trebizond from 1888 until his death, and was at one time Chamberlain to Pope Pius IX. We know nothing about the "42 years of Italian."

[25] Such was the reputation of the southern countries, especially during the first half of the nineteenth century, but according to John Pemble, in his excellent study of the subject entitled *The Mediterranean Passion* (1987), the really poor did not go to Mediterranean retreats, and the cheapness of Italy "was never such as to attract people who were not already disposed to go there." The reason, he says, was that "it was only luxuries that were cheap— palatial residences, carriages, wine, servants, boxes at the opera, and so on," while necessities other than food could be expensive. Even for the middle and upper classes, the cost of wood for heating was found to be excessive, and

even when the high cost of travel fell sharply by the final third of the century, the cost of living rose to offset it.

[26] Dunne tells this story in a passage from the memoir of Senator Cutting:

My friend [Cutting] was possibly decidedly interested in Ancient Greek, but he seldom mentioned that language. I had studied Ancient Greek three years under dumb professors and knew very little. I had studied Modern Greek in Rome, and with a professor from Athens, and I had learned sentences of tremendous use—in traveling around Athens. I had planned to visit Athens when I was called home in 1898. George Gissing wished me to go to Athens, a city he had visited. My friend was extremely amused at a letter sent to me in Rome by Professor Agonosthakos, aged *ninety-eighth year,* the letter in English and beginning:

"Mr. Gissing has spoken of you to me. I am a disciple of Homer and Socrates. Come to see me, my dear sir, at my hotel in Rome and I shall initiate you in the wonders of the Greek language."

[27] On March 18, 1898, Gissing received a card from a correspondent of the *Daily Telegraph,* and the next day recorded the interview: "Then to the [Hotel] Minerva, to call on the journalist Croke. Found him an unscrupulous interviewer, and had a stupid, annoying time; too weak to refuse, and obliged to talk platitudes." The published interview cannot be found.

[28] This is a sentiment which seems quite unlikely to have been expressed during Gissing's months with Dunne in Siena and Rome, a time which Dunne himself describes in these memoirs as perhaps the happiest in Gissing's life. The diary presents Gissing to us as totally occupied by his Dickens book in Siena, and after that too absorbed by his explorations in Calabria and then by his month in Rome with Wells, Doyle, Hornung, and Dunne to fall into such a state of depression. On the other hand, it is also clear that he was troubled by the news from Eliza Orme regarding his son and his wife's disturbing conduct, and by such attacks of illness as the one that prevented him from seeing a Papal Mass with Dunne, and about this time in his life Gissing became increasingly haunted by the perception (perhaps even desire) that he had not much longer to live, so that after all the sentiment is one which he doubtless expressed to Dunne. The mood is described in an undated entry in the *Commonplace Book:* "Life is over. No thought of horror, but of mere bewilderment. Mind soon turns from it in weariness. Nothing done. How I wasted the golden days! How strong I was! Think of my hardships, born *[sic]* without a groan. Life is meaningless." If, as we speculate, this passage dates from about

1900 (in the fall he was writing *The Private Papers of Henry Ryecroft,* where he expresses a similar feeling), it is nevertheless likely that it sums up sentiments which had developed in Gissing's mind over several years, and in fact his escape from a wretched family situation into the more joyous months in Rome might well have enhanced his regret about the wasted golden days.

[29] Justin Huntly McCarthy (1860–1936), dramatist, novelist, and historian, was the son of the more famous Justin McCarthy (1830–1912), the Irish historian and novelist, and the brother of Charlotte, with whom Gissing occasionally corresponded. On December 8, 1898, Gissing notes in his diary that he had received a copy of the son's *History of the United States,* and also a letter from Dunne and a copy of the *Baltimore Sun* containing a review of *The Town Traveller.* The interview with McCarthy has not been found, but Dunne worked for the *Sun* on his return from Italy in 1898, and it is possible that Dunne interviewed him in that city. But here Dunne mentions McCarthy in connection with Gissing, and if the interview took place in Rome, then doubtless it was Gissing who introduced the two men to each other.

[30] The mention of Wells here and at the beginning of this list is somewhat mysterious. There are a few slender references to Wells in the memoirs, and although in the memoir of Senator Cutting Dunne claims that he was the Wellses' guide around Rome whenever Gissing was too busy, he describes none of the anecdotes we are led to expect. It seems that Dunne either neglected them or he was here merely reminding himself that Wells was among the group of Gissing's friends in Rome.

[31] Henry Norman (1858–1939) was at this time the literary editor of the *Daily Chronicle,* and Gissing sent him the manuscript of "At the Grave of Alaric" in December of 1897. He had promised to give Gissing a letter of introduction to F. Marion Crawford, the American novelist living in Sorrento, but seems not to have done so. We do not know what Norman's "secret of success" was, but in writing to Clara Collet on January 14, 1896, Gissing makes a comment that seems to be somewhat disparaging: "Henry Norman, as you see, is going ahead in a line of vigorous ambition. There is already one Sir Henry [Irving], but some day we shall doubtless see another." On November 28, 1895, he had noted that "The Normans are back from their great campaign in the Balkhan peninsula—of which they will of course make a book," so perhaps the secret is to visit newsworthy places and write books about them, thus to get himself talked and written about. At any rate, Gissing seems to have thought of him as a man pushing his own self-confidence, who had many social contacts and sought the favor of influential men, and who actively aspired to knighthood. He did get a knighthood in 1906 and a baronetcy in 1915.

[32] Gissing's lifelong dislike and distrust of sports was a concern he shared with his German friend Eduard Bertz, who treated the subject formally at some length in his book on the newest sport of bicycling, *Philosophie des Fahrrads,* two years later. Bertz thought the greatest danger of an excessive cultivation of sports lay in the area of morals, making people "coarse and dull" and producing people who "cannot grasp the high value of humanity," and Gissing particularly agreed that the English may serve as a warning: "That a brutal power politics is met with the most lively sympathies in wide strata of the British people is not least a consequence of the barbarian instincts nurtured through boundless sports." Since Gissing seems to have impressed on Dunne the importance of his latest serious novel, *The Whirlpool,* he might have told him of the final chapter, in which Harvey Rolfe, whom Gissing used to satirize jingoist and colonialist attitudes, enlists sports to expose the philosophy: "See the spread of athletics. We must look to our physique, and make ourselves ready. Those Lancashire operatives, laming and killing each other at football, turning a game into a battle. For the milder of us there's golf—an epidemic. Women turn to cricket—tennis is too soft—and to-morrow they'll be bicycling by the thousand—they must breed a stouter race."

[33] As noted above, in note 37 for MS-A, Ilario Tacchi was an assistant librarian at the Biblioteca Angelica in Rome, who angered and humiliated Gissing by rebuking him for reading a newspaper in the library. Tacchi was a contentious man, having difficulties with the Director of the Library, who in the following November asked that he be transferred, suspended him for five days in December, and saw him transferred to the Biblioteca Lancisiana a year later. In the phrase which Dunne quotes here, Gissing is probably indulging in an elaborate pun on his name. *Tacco* (plural *tacchi*) means "heel," and *Salvatacco* (plural *salvatacchi*) means "heel-piece," so that Gissing seems to be calling him a "heel" or (if we vocally omit the space between the two words) a "heel-piece." Taken alone, however, *salva* means "saver," and the phrase would then mean "Saver Tacchi"—a sarcastic suggestion that the man, with his petty little rules, thought of himself as a kind of Savior of the Library. At any rate, Gissing was seriously angered by him, and it is this kind of paronomasial wit that Dunne means to convey—the exact meaning would be clear only with the vocal and facial expressions. It will occur to some readers that *salva* may be a typo for *salve,* in which case *salve Tacchi* would be an ironic expression of praise, as in "All hail to Tacchi for his bureaucratic solicitude." The final irony is that, ten years after this event, Tacchi published a report pleading for better conditions in Italian libraries.

[34] On February 22 Gissing received four copies of his Dickens book from Blackie's and gave one to Dunne. Two days later he recorded in his diary

"News that Zola—whose trial for libelling the generals in the Dreyfus affair ended yesterday—has been sentenced to a year's imprisonment and 3000 francs fine." Doubtless the event led to discussions with Dunne, and Gissing duly records his own opinion: "So far as I understand the matter, France seems sunk in infamy."

[35] An entry in the *Commonplace Book* may shed some light on this: "Yes, but the sad note in this 'Vie de Bohème'! The heart sinks now & then. This is the writing of a man who knew what poverty meant. That note I never find in Thackeray, for instance" (p. 35). Gissing refers here to Henri Murger (1822–1861), French author of *Scènes de la vie de Bohème* (published in installments between 1847 and 1849), source of the opera *La Bohème* (1896) by Giacomo Puccini.

[36] Gissing finished his Dickens book on November 5, 1897, in Siena, where he had first met Dunne, and three days later went to Rome, where Dunne was waiting for him. The two visited the Colosseum and other places the following morning, and then on the tenth Gissing left for Naples, whence he began his five weeks' tour of Calabria. He returned to Rome on December 15th, spending the following day with Dunne looking for a suitable room, and some of the Calabrian stories are told in Dunne's Article Two, printed above, where he explains the copper coin, but not the mounted police.

[37] This refers to Dickens's description of American men spitting on the floors of every bar-room and hotel passage, so that "the stone floor looks as if it were paved with open oysters. . . ." See note 13 to MS-A.

[38] This was the commemorative Mass of February 7 "for Pio Nono," who had died on that day ten years earlier. It is mentioned by Gissing in the diary, but although the ticket was given him by Dunne, it is not clear that Dunne was with him, and Gissing does not mention the black vestments.

[39] Gissing knew Greek and Latin, French, German, and Italian, and learned Spanish towards the end of his life.

[40] William II (1859–1941) came to power in 1888, and in a diary entry in June of that year Gissing expressed sadness at the death of Emperor Frederick III, adding: "I lament that a young savage has come to the throne." William was indeed a militaristic ruler with a passion for military display; his speeches constantly advocated German imperialism, and his military machine and complex system of alliances were contributing greatly to the events leading to World War I, a theme with which Gissing deals in *The Whirlpool* and *The Private Papers of Henry Ryecroft*. He also adopted an anti-British attitude during the South African wars, and Gissing was doubtless aware of his famous telegram to President Kruger of South Africa congratulating him on his suppression of

the famous Jameson Raid into the Transvaal. There are few specific references to him in either the letters or the diary, but Gissing shared the increasing British fear of impending war, and in 1903 he approved of "the vigorous line as regards Germany" taken in some articles by his former pupil, Austin Harrison, who was then a writer employed by the Reuters agency.

[41] Gissing visited the monastery at Monte Cassino on December 14–15, 1897.

[42] This is explained by an entry in the memoir of Senator Cutting: "My friend agreed with me that it was utterly stupid of the Catholic seminarians wandering round Rome and climbing the Seven Hills, to shout out, catching short breaths from exhaustion in climbing, such a sentence as this: *'De passionibus Jesu Christi'* and *'De incomprehensibilitus.'* And other long words—hard on hill climbers."

Appendices

A Radio Talk by Alfred Morang

[ALFRED MORANG (1901–1958), described in a newspaper story on his death as "one of Santa Fe's best-known and most colorful Bohemians," was an eccentric and an extremely versatile artist, painter, critic, musician, and writer, and a close friend of Erskine Caldwell. Born in Ellsworth, Maine, he went to Portland in 1929, where, in addition to teaching violin and art, he opened his own studio and organized showings of his own work and that of other artists. In 1937 he went for health reasons to Santa Fe, where he was sought out by "BB Dunne," as he was known there, who was curious about all things, and especially about eccentric people of great talent. Morang's principal medium was oils, but he worked extensively in watercolors, dry point, and etching, illustrating his own volume of poetry, some of Erskine Caldwell's work, and the poems of John Poda and Joseph Hoffman. His work was shown regularly at the Guggenheim Foundation for Non-Objective Painting and in various other galleries in Philadelphia, Boston, and several western cities, and is now undergoing a serious revival in Santa Fe, where his paintings draw increasingly high prices. As a critic and writer, he published stories and articles in more than a hundred magazines and newspapers. He also produced a weekly radio program entitled "The World of Art," including the broadcast dating from 1941 transcribed below. Alfred Morang died tragically in a fire at his home in Santa Fe at the age of fifty-six.]

Brian Ború Dunne, Collector of People
—by Alfred Morang

Brian Boru Dunne is a journalist, a commentator upon the human race, and a writer who uses words as if lifting many window shades upon the most unexpected aspects of life. He is a dynamic man with a face whittled sharp by observing great events and people. His voice is tense, and when interviewing some celebrity, his questions are unique for their meaning and brevity. The man Dunne is a phenomenon—half a magician who juggles reality into beauty, half a modern of the moderns able to write with the power which comes only from a great knowledge of literary and dramatic values.

He collects the words of great and near-great as a philatelist gathers rare stamps, and fastens them in the amazing album of his mind. His column, "Village Gossip," appearing in the *Santa Fe New Mexican,* is one of the most interesting features in the country and never fails to arouse attention and hold it from first line to last.

Dunne was born in Salt Lake City, Utah, son of the Chief Justice of Arizona under the administration of President Grant. At the age of ten he was publishing a monthly newspaper, setting the type by hand.[1] For five years he studied under the Benedictine Monks of St. Mary's in Belmont, North Carolina, and absorbed the knowledge of the past which was to stand him in such good stead in his varied career.[2] He studied languages against the background of European culture and delved into English, Latin, Ancient and Modern Greek with the late George Gissing, from 1897–1898. But he was never blinded by the glories of tradition. The most intense study served only to provide rungs in the ladder of knowledge upon which he was to mount to a profound grasp of modern life.

Dunne's newspaper experience has been an important part of his background. He was reporter and feature writer on the *Baltimore Sun* for three years; feature writer for the *Washington (D.C.) Times* under the late Frank Munsey; covered the White House at intervals, and acted as correspondent for the *Phoenix Gazette.* This journalist-writer has acted as correspondent for the four giants of

American journalism: Hearst, Pulitzer, Munsey and James Gordon Bennett.[3]

He entered the publicity field heading the newspaper bureau for the first San Diego Exposition in San Diego, California, and wrote daily for six hundred papers in the United States.[4] And while on the Reception Committee, he greeted visitors from the four corners of the earth, a fact which explains his ability to draw important news from people in all walks of life.[5]

For three years Dunne was private secretary to the late Cardinal Gibbons of Baltimore and, along with other secretarial work, cut his sermons of five thousand words to the one thousand necessary for publication in the *Baltimore Sun,* a technical feat of the greatest difficulty.[6] He was also secretary to the late U. S. Senator Bronson Cutting of New Mexico for twenty-three years, and for almost five years served in the same capacity to the late Archbishop Pitaval of the Roman Catholic archdiocese of Santa Fe, New Mexico.[7]

One of the highlights in Dunne's career was his refusal of an offer from Führer Hitler, made through Prince Louis Ferdinand of Prussia, to go to Berlin to write Nazi publicity for American, English and Irish newspapers.[8] But this act is typical of Dunne, whose belief in the greatness of his own country has never been weakened by his residence in ten countries and his uncommon knowledge of their political, social and economic problems.

Journalism and secretarial work have not claimed all of Brian Boru Dunne's attention. He studied short story technique with Hall and Nordhoff in the South Seas, and novel writing with George Gissing.[9] Dunne's book: *Cured: The Seventy Adventures of A Dyspeptic,* with a foreword by H. G. Wells, has sold for twenty-seven years; he has written five books.[10]

Dunne has adventured into many phases of human experience. He studied eye-strain—was appointed by the late Dr. George M. Gould of Atlantic City as his successor in broadcasting through the printed word the dangers of eye-strain.[11] And he studied the anomalies and curiosities of medicine with Dr. Gould and with the late Dr. Walter L. Pyle.[12]

Art and music are familiar to this versatile American. He studied piano and the German zither, and delved into the mysteries of the masters of painting under the guidance of important artists in Venice, Florence, Siena and Rome. He also studied Gregorian Chant with the Pères de Solesmes at Sablé-sur-Sarthe, France.[13]

Dunne toured throughout the country lecturing upon language study for the International Correspondence Schools of Scranton.[14] His interest in science is demonstrated by his study of the air-plane with its inventors, the Wright Brothers, to whom he gave their first French lessons by means of the phonograph. His preoccupation with science also led him to investigate the tetrahedral kite with the late Alexander Graham Bell, inventor of the telephone. He was possibly the first American to recognize the airplane as a formidable war weapon.

For the last thirty-two years, Brian Boru Dunne has lived in Santa Fe, New Mexico. In the Ancient City he has built or remodeled ten houses and apartments, and has followed his hobbies of collecting old watches, especially of foreign make which wind at the figure "one," and of accumulating some remarkable copper etchings.

To Dunne, Santa Fe offers the best all-year-round climate in the world, and is supreme in the number of its interesting residents and visitors.

As a reader, his choice is wide. He favors among English and American writers such masters as Shakespeare, Dickens and Jane Austen and such more modern writers as O. Henry and Erskine Caldwell, whom he considers one of the greatest of contemporary word-artists. He has read all of Brisbane's editorials,[15] all the works of H. G. Wells, Sinclair Lewis, Mencken and W. Somerset Maugham.

Dunne is a Roman Catholic in faith, and a political independent —having cast the first vote for William Jennings Bryan for President.

Brian Boru Dunne is one of the Southwest's greatest journalists, and a figure of unique interest. He may be summed up as being: a writer, and a man who possesses the genius of discrimination to a most remarkable degree.

Notes

¹ Dunne's father Edmund owned a printing press in the colony of San Antonio, Florida, which he had founded. In 1888 Brian, at the age of ten, printed a newspaper entitled *The Toy,* featuring local news and some advertising. In the issue of November 1 he printed an evaluation of it from an unknown source: "*The Toy* is a very neat and sprightly little paper published by Master Brian Dunne, of San Antonio, a wee bit of a little boy ten years of age. It is superior to many newspapers of far greater pretensions and is indeed a credit to its editor and the community in which it is published. Master Dunne writes and sets his own copy in first-class style. Should he live to reach more mature years, and we pray he may, and fulfills the brilliant promise of his boyhood, he will be one of the brightest ornaments in the sphere of journalism." In a "Valedictory" two weeks later, he explained that he must suspend publication, "our respected Governor [his father] informing us that we would have to bid our readers good bye for awhile and transfer the blaze of our intelligence to the classic halls of St. Mary's College, Gaston Co. N.C. Of course this will be a great thing for St. Mary's, but what will become of San Antonio Colony?"

² In 1889 Brian and his older brother Eugene, ages 10 and 13, were sent to St. Mary's College in Belmont, North Carolina, for a six-year course of study including a "full classical course . . . together with all other secular instruction there given of so-called extra studies or extra instruction which they or either of them may wish to receive. . . ." Brian graduated in 1893.

³ The first two of these names are the ones most commonly recognized today. William Randolph Hearst (1863–1951) took over the *San Francisco Examiner* from his father in 1887, and by the turn of the century owned several papers in the East, of which the most notable was the *New York Evening Journal.* Joseph Pulitzer (1847–1911) was also the owner of newspapers in the East, most importantly the *New York World,* which in fierce competition with Hearst became the first of the sensationalist "yellow journals." In neither case can we identify the papers for which Dunne wrote. Frank Andrew Munsey (1854–1925) was another enormously successful newspaper owner and editor, who was well known for buying numbers of magazines and newspapers in order to absorb or destroy them, on the principle that consolidation and combination were useful in decreasing competition. At one time his reputation was so widespread that, whenever a daily paper was rumored to be in distress, the slang expression in the newspaper world was "Let Munsey kill it." Among the papers he so destroyed were the *New York Morning Sun,* the *New York Press,* the *Mail Express,* the *Herald,* the *Baltimore Star,* and the *Philadelphia*

Times. He also bought and sold, after operating for a relatively short time, the *Boston Morning Journal,* the *Washington Times,* the *Baltimore American,* and the *Baltimore News,* earning for himself a reputation as a "dealer in dailies." At the time of his death he owned the extremely successful *New York Evening Sun* and the less successful *Evening Telegram.* We know from several sources that Dunne worked for the *Washington (D.C.) Times,* in which appeared his celebrated interview with Mark Twain (see introduction).

James Gordon Bennett (1841–1918) was an editor and capitalist, trained at his father's newspaper, the *New York Herald,* of which he became managing editor in 1866 and chief executive officer a year later. He had a penchant for surrounding himself with talented men, including Henry M. Stanley, whom he assigned to cover the British Army in Abyssinia; so impressed was Bennett with his correspondent's reports from Africa that in 1869 he sent Stanley to look for the British explorer David Livingstone, yielding a story that won fame for Bennett and his paper. We do not know which of his papers Dunne wrote for. Dunne mentioned him in a 1906 interview of John Temple Graves, whom he likened to Samuel L. Clemens as being "nice men" with a "kindly feeling," willing "to take their own medicine," adding that "They are totally different from James Gordon Bennett in this regard."

[4] This was the San Diego Panama Exposition of 1915/16, celebrating the opening of the Panama Canal and the expectation that San Diego would become a major port. Dunne was the head of the news bureau there, which was designed to give maximum coverage to the Exposition to boost the fame of San Diego, and sent out daily reports to newspapers all over the country. Dunne had probably been sponsored for the position as a political expediency by Bronson Cutting, who in the senatorial race was on a collision course with Territorial Congressman A. W. (Bull) Andrews, with whom Dunne had worked ardently on the problem of New Mexican statehood. At the Panama Exposition Dunne got on so well with Theodore Roosevelt, who had made the Panama Canal possible, that Cutting asked him to invite the ex-president to stop at Santa Fe on his way back east.

[5] This was at Santa Fe, where a Reception Committee was designed to greet and accommodate the many celebrated figures from around the world who came there, and Dunne was unofficially known as the "town greeter."

[6] For Cardinal Gibbons, see headnote to Appendix 2.

[7] John Baptiste Pitaval succeeded Archbishop Bourgade in 1909, becoming the last in a continuous succession of French archbishops of Santa Fe. He retired because of poor health in 1918. According to an obituary of Dunne, he was a private secretary to Archbishop Pitaval from 1909 to 1912.

⁸ This Prince was not a member of the de Croÿ family, but a Hohen-zollern, grandson of Kaiser Wilhelm II, German Emperor from 1888 to 1918, when he was forced to abdicate during the turmoil of World War I. He fled the country, and eventually settled with his family in Doorn, Holland. At first Morang's claim here seemed to us to be somewhat fanciful, but since everything else Morang says can be verified elsewhere, we asked Brian Boru II to try tracking it down in his father's papers. What he found, among other items, was the following cablegram dated December 14, 1933, from Brian Ború Dunne in Santa Fe to the "Secretary of His Imperial Majesty the Kaiser" in Doorn, Holland: "AT THE REQUEST OF THE KAISER S GRANDSON PRINCE LOUIS FERDINAND MAY I INTERVIEW HIS IMPERIAL MAJESTY IN ABOUT TWO WEEKS?" We do not know whether the interview took place, but according to the Kaiser's biographer, the grandson, after finishing his studies in 1929, "had then gone on an extended trip through North and South America. He worked for a time on the assembly line of the Ford Motor Company, had met people of all walks of life, was reputedly liberal and intelligent and cultured; he had even come to know President Franklin D. Roosevelt personally." It is certain that the Prince visited the famous health center of Santa Fe, perhaps even at the suggestion of the de Croÿ family, with whom Dunne had kept up a friendly relationship, and that he was acquainted with Senator Cutting and with Dunne, who conducted an interview with him. In a 1946 letter to Col. Elmer Brown Mason, Dunne recalled some of the events of that time: "It appears that Prince Louis Ferdinand of Prussia had asked Senator Cutting to let me go to Berlin for a year to do publicity work and had asked Senator Cutting to caution me against American cocktails before meals—as his adviser, the ex-Kaiser had told him this was a dietetic sin and 'chemically unsound.'" In 1933, when the Kaiser called his grandson back from America, the Hohen-zollerns were supporting Hitler under the illusion that he would restore the monarchy, and "the princes lent themselves to Nazi propaganda displays, fur-ther dignifying the Nazi thugs by their presence and tacit approval" (Walter Henry Nelson, *The Soldier Kings: The House of Hohenzollern* [Putnam's Sons, 1970], p. 444). The anti-Nazi resistance groups in Germany, who were not well-known figures nationally, needed a more visible leader or a figurehead who could give them legitimacy, but were so extremely skeptical of the suit-ability of the Kaiser and the Crown Prince for their cause that they consid-ered Prince Louis Ferdinand. When the Prince returned from America, the Nazis tried to win his allegiance, but his eyes "had been opened and his mind enlarged during years of travel, and he refused any association with the Nazi leaders." In his letter to Col. Mason, Dunne recollected some further events before the Prince was recalled to Germany: "I remember the first visit of

Prince Ferdinand to Santa Fe—he brought a letter from Governor La Follette of Wisconsin stating that 'in case of a restoration of the Hohenzollerns' Ferdinand was to ascend the throne. As I remember, Ferdinand and Senator Cutting discussed the future of the Hohenzollerns *'between piano duets'* at Senator Cutting's residence, Siete Burros, in Santa Fe, and Senator Cutting told me that Ferdinand seemed to have assurance from the ex-Kaiser of the following program." That is, the Kaiser was to receive a call from Hitler about the need of a monarchy, he would renounce it and pass it on to the Crown Prince, who would also decline it, "and pass on the crown to Ferdinand, the Kaiser's choice." "I discussed the plan with Ferdinand," Dunne added, "and he asked me to call up 'the old man' (the ex-Kaiser) at Doorn by telephone and offer friendly greetings from Santa Fe." In 1949 Dunne recollected another encounter with the Prince during his editorship of the newspaper: "We ran a picture of Grand Duchess Kyra of Russia with her husband, Prince Louis Ferdinand, when they were here on their world-tour-honeymoon."

⁹ Since Dunne spent only a few months with Gissing in Italy and less than half a year with Hall and Nordhoff in Tahiti, it may seem a bit hyperbolical to say that Dunne "studied with" either Gissing or Nordhoff—although in his letter to H. G. Wells of January 21, 1933, he identifies himself as a "pupil of George Gissing," and there can be little doubt that these topics were matters of conversation. It seems more reasonable to say, as Morang does above, that Dunne "delved into" the novel as well as the several languages with Gissing during their five months together in Italy. The delving, however, might have been more thorough than we know, since the teacher/student aspect was certainly implicit in their relationship, even though Dunne does not stress that in the memoirs. Charles Bernard Nordhoff (1887–1947) was a writer born in London of American parentage, author of *The Fledgling* (1919), *The Pearl Lagoon* (1924), *Picaro* (1924), and *The Derelict* (1928). He co-authored a number of books with James Norman Hall (b. 1887), an American writer from Iowa who served in the Escadrille Lafayette in 1917 and lived in Tahiti from 1920. Among the works in collaboration were *The Lafayette Flying Corps* (1920), *Faery Lands of the South Seas* (1921), *Falcons of France* (1929), a trilogy narrating the story of the ship *Bounty* (*Mutiny on the Bounty*, 1932; *Men against the Sea*, 1934; *Pitcairn's Island*, 1934), *The Hurricane* (1935), *The Dark River* (1936), *Botany Bay* (1941), and *Men without Country* (1942). Their short stories were extremely popular. In Tahiti, Dunne and Frank Blair, the Chicago stockbroker turned treasure hunter, roomed on the second floor of the Tiare Hotel, at the opposite end from Hall and Nordhoff, and thus could observe them and get to know them. Later he made the following entry in an unpublished book: "Hall & Nordhoff, the famous South Sea Island literary firm, did their work in

the forenoon. Hall wrote on a portable typewriter, Nordhoff with a pen. They wrote for five hours each a day." Dunne and Hall corresponded for several years.

[10] A witty exposé of American medical practice near the turn of the century, *Cured!* was published in 1914 and reprinted in 1937, enabling us to date Morang's broadcast as 1941. Later Dunne sent a copy of his book to George Bernard Shaw, who wrote him a brief note dated April 24, 1947: "Thank you for the book. I wrote a British counterpart to it myself years ago, called Doctors' Delusions. . . . My complaint (headaches once a month or so) was only an excuse for sampling the treatments. They ceased when I was 70. All the practitioners I had consulted at once claimed to have cured me. G.B.S." Dunne appears to have nearly completed another book, to be entitled "Popes, Pugilists and Presidents," for which a typed list of topics is in the Van Pelt Library at the University of Pennsylvania, and for which he solicited endorsements from famous writers, but *Cured!* is the only one that appears in the Library of Congress catalog. However, it seems likely that he wrote other books that may have been published locally, perhaps by the New Mexican Printing Company owned by his friend Senator Bronson Cutting: in 1948, H. Allen Smith, whom Dunne described as "another of those damn Eastern writers," noted that people were talking about his "sort of daffy book about dieting." In a letter to him of April 21, 1931, John D. Rockefeller wrote "I note that you are sending me one of your books on diet." And according to a brief notice in the *New Mexico Sentinel* (March 9, 1938), Dunne was to spend a week in Hollywood "to meet a moving picture producer," and on his return was to write a book on New Mexico's "Old timers," famous Southwestern characters such as Charley Siringo. Indeed, Dunne corresponded with Cecil B. de Mille after a visit on a train ride to Pasadena.

[11] George Milby Gould (1848–1922) was a physician specializing in ophthalmology, who set up his practice in Philadelphia in 1888 and devised the cemented bifocal lens. According to the *DAB* he had a tempestuous professional life, developing theories on the effects of eyestrain on physical and mental health, but expressing them in such belligerent terms that they were regarded as false and radical in his time, though later widely accepted. He had a literary bent, and befriended Lafcadio Hearn, whom he enticed from the West Indies to his own home in Philadelphia, and in 1908 wrote an analytical volume entitled *Concerning Lafcadio Hearn* in response to Elizabeth Bisland's uncritical biography. With Walter Lytle Pyle he wrote the *Cyclopedia of Practical Medicine and Surgery* in 1900. He wrote six volumes of *Biographic Clinics* (1903–1909), in which he interpreted such writers as De Quincey, Carlyle, and George Eliot in the light of his theory of eyestrain. In 1901 he wrote *Sug-*

gestions to Medical Writing, with a view to setting up a school of medical journalism. Moving to Philadelphia from Salina, Ohio, he practiced there from 1888 to 1908 and from 1908 to 1911 in Ithaca, New York, where he knew Dunne. In his memoir of Cutting, Dunne wrote that the senator would "listen with rapt attention to letters Gould wrote me because Gould believed my book *Cured* would do a world of good in battling eyestrain. Later my friend was impressed with Gould on reading 'Anomalies and Curiosities in Medicine,' now a 15 dollar book. Gould and Pyle wrote it." In a letter to Wells of June 15, 1912, when Dunne had just finished *Cured!,* he said that "Dr. Gould the famous ophthalmist & litterateur is trying to have it run serially. He is going to ask the *Saturday Evening Post* to do this, then he hunts a publisher in this country."

[12] Walter Lytle Pyle (1871–1921) was an ophthalmologist born in Philadelphia, an assistant surgeon to Dr. Conrad Berens at the Wills Hospital, and an editorial writer in medical literature. With Gould he wrote *A Compend of the Diseases of the Eye* (1899) and the *Cyclopedia of Practical Medicine and Surgery* (1900). He was editor of the *International Medical Magazine* in 1898.

[13] Solesmes is a small town south of Le Mans, and near Sablé-sur-Sarthe, with a distinguished Benedictine monastery dating from the 11th century. The building was sacked by the English in the 15th century and the monks were expelled during the Revolution and later, but in the mid-19th century it became the head of French Benedictine houses, and the abbot Dom Guéranger restored Benedictine life and was instrumental in reviving Gregorian chant there and the study of it, for which the abbey is famous. In the letter to Col. Mason, mentioned in note 8 above, Dunne spoke of this monastery in connection with Mrs. Justine Ward, the sister of his friend Senator Bronson Cutting: "Later I went to Europe and Mrs. Ward talked of publicity work on Gregorian chant in Rome. It appeared she had 500 schools in Italy teaching Gregorian chant. I spent a week listening to the chants by the Pères de Solesmes at Sablé, northwest of Paris." In an undated press release about Guglielmo Marconi's visit to Santa Fe, sent to the *Albuquerque Morning Journal,* Dunne said that "Senator Cutting called on Senator Marconi, who is a friend of Mrs. Justine B. Ward, sister of Senator Cutting, and founder of eight hundred schools in Italy for teaching Mrs. Ward's method of Gregorian chant."

[14] The ICS, still headquartered in Scranton, Pennsylvania, was founded in the 1890s to be of service in qualifying miners for administrative posts, but expanded rapidly, establishing various schools in communications, including the use of the phonograph in the study of languages.

[15] Arthur Brisbane (1864–1936) was the most successful newspaper editor and the most popular editorial writer of his time, of whom it was said

that no man in the history of journalism was read more widely and continuously. He was so successful as New York editor of the *Sun* that Joseph Pulitzer brought him over to the *New York World,* which under his direction became the first of the sensationalist "yellow journals" and the world leader in circulation, making its owner very rich. Under his editorship, too, the *Sunday World* became even more flashy and lurid in competition with William Randolph Hearst's *Evening Journal,* and when Pulitzer prevented him from running editorials on the front page, he joined forces with Hearst, increasing the circulation of the *Journal* from 40,000 to 325,000 within seven weeks, and for the next forty years became Hearst's ardent supporter. The *Journal*'s circulation went over a million as Brisbane indulged in jingoist propaganda, such as inflammatory and deliberately false stories of atrocities in Cuba and the Philippines, leading to the Spanish-American war. After the war his attacks on President McKinley became vicious, even including articles on the benefits of assassination, but when the President was actually shot he wrote nothing but admiring words about that "beloved leader." For this kind of contradiction, and for other reasons, he was accused of easy reversability, of having an adjustable conscience, and of turning editorials into platitudinous homilies dubbed "brisbanalities." He wrote deliberately for the uneducated, criticizing one of his editors for writing editorials that made people think—"Editorials," he said, "should make people think they think." But readers were attracted by his affirmative tone, his simple clarity, and his terse and provocative style, using short sentences and short paragraphs often consisting of one or two such sentences. He wrote and dictated with great speed and facility, often writing a column in fifteen minutes, speaking into dictaphones in his limousine and on airplanes and trains. Dunne had known Brisbane at least casually, and when he wrote of him after Brisbane's death, he carefully stressed that kind of personal observation: "At the top of his career as a writer, acclaimed as the greatest columnist in the English language, the late Arthur Brisbane remained humble. He would correct his typed column with a heavy pencil, and often submitted to FIVE corrections at the home office. . . . At times Brisbane was so hard pressed to get out his column . . . he had to write on the train and telegraph the comments to the home office—the 'broadcasting' division. Brisbane was once asked by a New Mexico newspaperman whether he was traveling from Chicago to Los Angeles in 'a private railway car, filled with great writers.' He replied: 'No; I might feel out of place.'" Brisbane, in fact, once admitted that "anyone who writes as rapidly as I . . . can never be a great writer."

APPENDIX 2

Brian Ború Dunne, "Cardinal Gibbons and Longevity"

[JAMES, CARDINAL GIBBONS (1834–1921) was ordained in 1861, became secretary to the archbishop of Baltimore in 1865, vicar apostolic of North Carolina in 1868, bishop of Richmond in 1872, and in 1877 the ninth Archbishop of Baltimore at the age of forty-three. He was created cardinal in 1886, and was the first chancellor of the Catholic University of America in Washington, D.C. He was vitally interested in the growth of the Catholic church within the American democracy. He insisted on the oneness of American citizenship and obligations among all people, opposed German extremists, tried to bring harmony to the lives of Catholics, and was one of the most outspoken supporters of the separation of Church and State. The Cardinal was a personal friend of three presidents, and was particularly successful in his relations with Protestants. His book *The Faith of Our Fathers,* an apology for Catholicism written for conservative Protestants, sold over a million copies. Dunne was at his service at the turn of the century, when Gibbons had to deal with the controversy between quarrelling groups of Catholics of different national backgrounds, chiefly Irish and German, for which a man of Dunne's background might be useful to him. The role of "personal secretary" was an informal one, including the professional job of editing the sermons for publication, but as a personal friend Dunne spent many evenings with the Cardinal discussing a range of topics including Vatican politics. Dunne wrote the following article on the death of the Cardinal, and we offer it here as a reflection of the conversations and a sample of Dunne's journalistic style and his observation of details.]

Cardinal Gibbons and Longevity
—*By Brian Boru O'Dunne*

In these days in America, when prominent men, oppressed by business worries or domestic infelicity, break down at the age of forty, we wonder how a man holding such a responsible position as Cardinal Gibbons could reach 87.

One of the Cardinal's old friends, who lectures occasionally on health at Battle Creek Sanitarium, wrote me this week:

"Cardinal Gibbons, who lived to be 87, was never sick until shortly before his death. He ate carefully and liked apples for dessert. He was not tense nor nervous and *he did not worry*. His colon was perfect; his stomach was delicate—but he knew enough to eat light meals and shun all excess."

I knew the Cardinal very well and I used to call on him every evening at 9. We often discussed the secret of health, the secrets of longevity.

The Cardinal opposed America's favorite vice of *heavy meat eating*. He exhorted me to shun beefsteaks and pork chops, and the like. He recommended the white meat of chicken or a squab—if one had to eat meat. He advised me, then suffering from nervous dyspepsia, to keep away from all doctors and to map out a sensible course of living.

The Cardinal objected to heavy and late dinners—excessive food.

His Eminence objected to reading books and magazines and newspapers on moving trains and in street cars—America's favorite sport. The Cardinal believed this reading with jerky movements was a strain on the eyes.

He said to me in 1905 that he had had dyspepsia for forty

years. I later heard the prelate got his dyspepsia from rough and terrible meals while he was a missionary bishop—a vicar apostolic —in North Carolina.

The Cardinal believed in the simplest and cheapest of exercises, now so much neglected in America. He said: "Walk an hour or two each day in the fresh air." The prelate himself set an example in this regard—he walked daily along Baltimore's streets.

M. Phillips Price, member of the English parliament and distinguished London journalist, says in his new book "America Old and New," written following a tour across the U.S.A., that "nobody walks in the states."

The Cardinal advised me not to read at night—under artificial light. That too was a strain on the eyes of a dyspeptic, of a nervous dyspeptic particularly.

And the prelate's final note of advice was: "Be cheerful."

I shall quote a note from one of the Cardinal's friends, who has been reading Good Health magazine since 1893, when he saw a copy at the World's Fair in Chicago:

> "I have studied the secret of perfect health for 44 years. The fundamental secret of health and longevity is intestinal drainage, which may be effected by various methods."

This health enthusiast sees intestinal stasis—we call it by the plainer word, constipation—in health magazines as the characteristic of people who are enervated, who need relaxation and rest as much as correct food. He adds: "These people are usually tense and of the nervous, race-horse type. The placid, bovine man of the draft horse type is seldom constipated."

One of the leading medical writers and doctors in the Rocky Mountain Region says his secret of curing constipation is to cut down his food allowance 50 per cent until he overcomes the difficulty.

Others use well-chewed nuts, fruits and vegetables to give bulk—to cure constipation. There is too much mushy food, with all rough stuff taken out.

Perhaps the best cure of all is to drink cold water in the early morning, eat some ripe raw fruit and walk a half mile or mile—an hour before breakfast. But dyspeptics must be careful about raw fruit, especially about that half-ripened stuff that is shipped out of California—if we may believe eminent medical men.

The Boy Scouts' manual deals with constipation, its cause and cure, and perhaps the New Americans will be able to battle with this distressing, life-shortening plague.

If Cardinal Gibbons had not had the worries and responsibilities of a great prelate, he might have lived to be a hundred years. Worry, not work, kills, as Osler said. Of 300 popes of Rome, who led much the same life in the Vatican they had led in their diocese, only five reached the age of 80. Leo XIII managed to "limp along rather feebly to 94," but he *ate nuts like a bird*. I saw him take breakfast once, in 1898, after a service in the Sistine Chapel. I think his meal was about four mouthfuls.

One of the great secrets of longevity, I should say, is to avoid falls in extreme old age. We are always hearing of some old man or some old woman falling, tripping, and breaking a bone. And then dying of pneumonia.

A good plan at the age of 90 or 100, it seems to me, would be to go to bed . . . . and stay there. With the radio, with wonderfully improved electric lights, making reading easier than in 1905 when Cardinal Gibbons warned against night reading, life might prove a comfort. And there are moving pictures for the home.

The secret of longevity, however, is the secret Cardinal Gibbons discovered and used: *The Simple Life.*

I myself—and I am 59 years of age—find perfect health when I shun: alcohol, tobacco, heavy meats, coffee and tea. And I do not take serums, and I do not take medicine.

APPENDIX 3

Brian Ború Dunne, "'My Ten Rules of Oratory,' by William Jennings Bryan, as Dictated to Brian Boru Dunne"

[William Jennings Bryan (1860–1925) was a lawyer and a populist politician, elected as U.S. Representative from Lincoln, Nebraska, 1891–95, but defeated for the Senate in 1894. He was an ardent supporter of the silver forces in Congress, arguing for the free and unlimited coinage of silver, became the most popular speaker in the drive to control the Democratic national convention at Chicago in 1896, and at the convention his famous "cross of gold" speech won him the presidential nomination. In a strenuous and bitterly fought contest, he lost to William McKinley in 1896 and again in 1900, and finally to William H. Taft in 1908. In 1912 his switch of allegiance to Woodrow Wilson so far helped in that nomination and election that Wilson made him secretary of state, and in the following months he was influential in the enactment of Wilson's reform legislation. He fought for such causes as woman suffrage and public knowledge of newspaper ownership, and his immense personal charm and golden voice made him the greatest orator of his day. He was a Presbyterian and a fundamentalist, addressed legislatures for measures against the teaching of evolution, and argued for the prosecution in the famous Scopes Trial. He won the case, but died five days after the trial.]

My Ten Rules of Oratory
by William Jennings Bryan
as dictated to Brian Boru Dunne

My first rule for a successful orator is to have something to say. Some of the world's greatest orators had no voice whatsoever ("Did you by any chance refer to John Temple Graves?" Mr. Bryan was silent).

In order to have something to say the would-be orator should read avidly. He should read the best works ("Did you, Mr. Bryan, by any chance refer to Dr. Elliott's five foot shelf of books?" Mr. Bryan was silent).

In order to be a great orator, the speaker should have information. I think I got it by my travels, by my study, by my experience, by my contacts.

Mr. Gladstone was a great orator. He was a very well educated man. He conveyed power of conviction when he spoke. Roscoe Conkling was a great orator. As for Conkling, he had an emotional power that was priceless. That cannot be developed immediately. That comes from within the man. If you would like to be a great orator, kindly study the career of Mr. Conkling. By study of the great orators you might learn something.

My second rule of oratory is, to go on the stage and avoid an echo. An orator should never speak when he is under a serious handicap. People have criticized me for walking around the stage during my orations. I never walked on the stage through nervousness. I did it to avoid an echo. I am not a nervous man. I never was nervous in my life. I realized that I must get the best effect. My audience depends upon me to give them a perfect oration ("Mr. Bryan, you happen to be the greatest elocutionist in the world. I never heard you when you didn't give a perfect oration").

My third rule is, to study the face of some person in the audience. I usually pick out a man who seems interested in my discourse. Invariably I speak to him, and to him alone. I try to convince him. There is a sea of faces. I pay no attention to the others. Some orators criticize my idea, but I feel I have met with a measure of success by this plan. You would undoubtedly be amused to know how much influence that one face has upon my discourse.

To an orator I would say the fourth rule is, have a good memory (I said, "Mr. Bryan, you have the most wonderful memory in the world. I heard you deliver a speech in Baltimore that took fourteen columns of the *Baltimore American* to report accurately. No single reporter could report it, so they employed a staff. It was one of the most remarkable feats of journalism to take your speech, which started early in the night, and which ended late at night, and have it in the mail edition at two A.M." Mr. Bryan again smiled and said "Oh, I have made much longer speeches than that. Tell me, Dunne, how long was that speech?" I said "fourteen columns." He replied: "Twenty columns is nothing to me.")

My fifth rule of oratory is to have good health. It is a great effort to speak to a great audience. The world is looking at you. It is usually late at night. You are under a great mental strain. If you are a great orator this means nothing to you, but you have to have good health to stand the strain. ("Mr. Bryan, when I heard you in Baltimore deliver the most wonderful speech I ever heard in my life, you had already spoken twenty-two times that day." Mr. Bryan replied "If you know the secret of oratory, the delivery of twenty-two short speeches would not tire you. The only thing that tires me is lack of response. Everywhere I traveled that day I received an enthusiastic response." I said to Mr. Bryan "You are such a wonderful orator that farmers and their wives sat in blankets through the cold of the night to hear the matchless speaker." Mr. Bryan replied "I thank you for the compliment. We will now go on.")

("Mr. Bryan, is it true that you have the most wonderful voice in the world? How did you develop it?" "I have already told you that voice is not all important, but it helps an orator. Correct living, wonderful heredity, life on the farm might develop a good voice. Of course, lungs are important. As I have already stated, a voice in oratory is secondary. It is the words you use, the subject back of it that counts.")

(Mr. Bryan, is it a fact that you took singing lessons to develop your wonderful voice? "Now, Mr. Dunne, you are touching upon a subject that is very dear to me. I really am a disappointed man. I wished to be a grand opera singer." I said "You, the world's greatest elocutionist, are jealous of Caruso?" Mr. Bryan replied "I will only say this, I wish I were a grand opera singer.")

(I said, "Did you ever sing?" Mr. Bryan replied "Yes, in the chorus of a church. I never sang any other place.")

(Then I gave Mr. Bryan a dissertation on grand opera singing. I told him I had been a music critic on an eastern paper; that I had studied the voices of the world's greatest singers; I had written press notices about Nordica and others; I had come to the conclusion that a grand opera voice is as rare as a grand romance; it just can't be done. God gives you, or he does not give you, what is called the sound box in your mouth. You can't produce great singing notes if you haven't the music box. I said to Bryan "Just because you are the greatest elocutionist in the world doesn't mean you are a Caruso, and you might as well know it." Mr. Bryan replied "Isn't that strange?")

My seventh rule would be gestures. I believe in simplicity of gestures. The gesture must be natural. Don't make a gesture unless it is called for by your statement. ("Mr. Bryan, why do you make so few gestures in your discourses?" Mr. Bryan answered "I don't need them.")

My eighth secret of oratory, which I am willing to give to the American public and to some of my English friends across the seas who might learn diction from America, is this, when you begin an address, kindly speak in a low voice. Then ascend gradually. In that way you may achieve a climax. I cannot tell you how sad are the orators in colleges of America. They start in a high key and there is no climax. Their voices crack. In my college days I heard many of these orators—collegiate orators—who started in a high key, only to find their voices cracking when they tried to achieve a climax.

Of course, an orator should be properly clothed, both men and women appreciate a properly dressed speaker. ("Mr. Bryan, is it a fact that you invariably send your dress suit to a dry cleaners two hours before your discourse, and isn't it a fact that you did that in Baltimore to get two hours sleep?" Mr. Bryan replied, "A little rest before an oration is beneficial, but after all, an orator should appear at his best.")

Tenth rule. An orator should finish one word before he begins another. Never have I been so irritated as to listen to the sloppy English of so-called American speakers. When you are on the stage delivering an oration, address, or a few remarks at a banquet, you should speak every word evenly. Don't slur your English. The audience is entitled to hear what you have to say in clean-cut phrases. One of the great troubles in America today is this: People unbalance their words. They deliver a beautiful sentence and mar its ending. They seem to be in a hurry. That is not the trait of an orator. If your words have any meaning, they should be delivered evenly. I have always tried to do that, and I think with a measure of success.

As to the Cross of Gold speech, which made Bryan nationally famous in less than two hours, I have heard stories, through Mark Sullivan, Washington correspondent of the New York Herald Tribune, that Bryan had delivered that speech all over the state of Illinois, and other states, two hundred times before the great success in the Chicago convention. Mr. Bryan again smiled when I suggested that he had had elaborate preparation before making his colossal success in the Democratic national convention. His smile said to me "I don't think we'll go into that."

There is another story going around that Mrs. Bryan assisted William Jennings Bryan in the preparation of his speeches. I don't think Mr. Bryan paid very much attention to these rumors. He intimated to me that he wrote his own speeches, memorized them and delivered them on his own.

In my conversation with Mr. Bryan he told me there was one man in the United States he admired, and his name was Lindsay

Johnston, an editor of a Georgia paper, because Mr. Johnston had voted for Mr. Bryan in a convention 78 times. Mr. Bryan, in his conversation with me, prized political loyalty as the greatest virtue of the American voter. When he heard I was writing an article about him, Mr. Bryan, for Mr. Johnston's newspaper, he said practically this: "You may stay in this room just as long as you like. Ask me any questions you like."

Presuming on this munificence, I then asked Mr. Bryan a very unfortunate question. I said "Is it true that you are moving the State of Nebraska into the State of Texas?"

Mr. Bryan's whole manner changed. His brow became clouded; his smile vanished; he remained silent for the minute. Then he spoke as follows: "This question is very annoying to me. It also annoys Mrs. Bryan. I don't like it. I don't think a newspaperman should ask me such a question. Especially a nice newspaper man, as you seem to be."

I replied "I don't see why I should annoy Mr. Bryan. After all, you have been very generous to give me so much time, and so much information."

The subject got around to stories about Bryan. He suddenly became more amicable, and he wished to know what people were saying about him. I told him I just had luncheon with the son of a Congressman who sat next to him in Congress. "What did he say about me?" asked Bryan. I replied "Do you wish to know exactly what he said?" "Yes," said Bryan, with a smile.

"He said 'My father, who sat in the seat next to Bryan in Congress, used to remark at night, after a session of Congress, that William Jennings Bryan had the damndest gift of gab given by God to a human being.'" Mr. Bryan again smiled, and made no comment whatsoever.

Bryan told me then his secret in handling the press. When ten reporters wished to interview him, said Bryan, "I believe it is a good rule to take out your watch, give each of them ten minutes. After all a reporter is entitled to interview me when I am alone. I do not believe in collective interviewing."

Bryan felt that he had been badly treated by the voters of the United States, but he was willing to run for president as often as they wished to nominate him. He seemed to have the idea that some day he would be elected president. When I saw him, he was ready to run again if the voters wished him to head the ticket. There is nothing in defeat, according to Bryan. The secret of success is try and try again. As for criticism of his course, Mr. Bryan felt that when you go on the ticket you must expect bitter opposition from certain classes. The great political leader can expect nothing else.

Bryan's greatest delight was to speak to people. He felt he had a message. The adulation he received up to the hour of his death convinced him he had the people with him.

I saw Mr. Bryan arrive in Baltimore in or about the year 1900. He stepped off the train, and it required sixteen policemen to escort him safely to his carriage. There were only five motor cars in Baltimore at that time, so far as I know. One of the rare motor cars was owned by Mrs. Isaac E. Emmerson, wife of the inventor of Bromo Selzer. As far as I know, this motor car was not at the depot to welcome Mr. Bryan. So the great Commoner had to trust his locomotion to a carriage. With a great deal of difficulty the sixteen policemen prevented Mr. Bryan from being mauled by a mob of admirers. A few years later—quite a few years—I saw Mr. Bryan arrive in Santa Fe, and I was one of twelve men who met him at the depot. Mr. Bryan was then delivering an address at the Scottish Rite Cathedral auditorium in behalf of Liberty Bonds. I said to Mr. Bryan, "You look the picture of health, you who have been through so many political battles, have emerged unscarred." Bryan replied, "I have just had a wonderful sleep in a quiet village called Lamy. Mr. Dunne, have you ever heard of a place called Lamy?"

I replied "That place is named after the Archbishop of Santa Fe, our first Roman Catholic Archbishop. It strikes me as a rather restful place, but a little more restful than that town of Gallup, where you delivered a speech the other night." Bryan chuckled. He was in splendid humor. I had just received a report that in Gallup Mr. Bryan's temper was slightly ruffled when a lawyer named A. T. Hannett had introduced him to a large and admiring Democratic audience as "One of the greatest orators in the world." It would seem that Mr. Hannett, a leading Democrat, inadvertently had stepped on the toes of the great Commoner, and according to reports, Mr. Bryan showed an unpardonable burst of anger by rejoining "This is not an oratorical contest," or words to that effect.

Of course in my conversations with Mr. Bryan I never suggested there was another orator in the world that was his equal. Maybe that is why I got along so well with him. I have the impression, from conversations with Mr. Bryan, that he felt that as an elocutionist and an orator he possibly was supreme. Countless people said so. I never heard of anybody telling Bryan that he wasn't. When I asked him for his secrets of oratory, he replied with the assurance of a master. He never said "I may be wrong," and he never used the word "possibly." I asked him as a simple reporter, speaking through the press to America, "What are the ten secrets of your success?" I told him that I had never heard such a beautiful oration in my life as he delivered in Baltimore. I told him that his Prince of Peace oration—that is, excerpts—were on my phonograph and listened to by admiring friends in both parties. He undoubtedly heard that a great Jesuit made this remark about his oratory: "I have to follow my rule. I am a Jesuit. I think I'm a public speaker. I have spoken from the pulpit for forty years. In order to improve my knowledge of oratory I went down to the depot in Albuquerque to spend five minutes listening to the style of oratory of William Jennings Bryan. My conscience permitted me to spend five minutes. I fear I have sinned grievously. I stayed two hours listening to that damned man. He's the most wonderful orator in the world. He could make you think black is white. He could paint a panacea for the ills of mankind. Positively I have never heard a speaker with such magnetism."

When I was twenty years of age I was bowled over by Bryan's speech in Baltimore, and I took a copy—verbatim copy—of his address published in the *Baltimore American*—my paper, the *Baltimore Sun,* wouldn't run fourteen columns—to the then managing editor of the *Baltimore Sun,* Mr. Haines. In the introduction to the address of Mr. Bryan, the *Baltimore American* stated editorially that Bryan had repeated threadbare arguments, which he had spread all over the United States. The *Baltimore American* suggested Mr. Bryan had brought nothing new to Baltimore. Mr. Haines, about 70 years of age, remarked coldly "The arguments are threadbare alright."

Mr. Bryan had a very strange habit at banquets to take his champagne glass and turn it down long before there was any popping corks. One of his greatest admirers, a United States Senator, asked me "Can't you get him out of that habit?" I replied "Mr. Bryan never drank a drop of anything stronger than grape juice in his life. He considers it improper to sit in front of foaming champagne." (I heard that Bryan refused to deliver an address at the Waldorf Astoria Hotel because there was dancing in the adjoining room. Champagne and dancing disturbed Mr. Bryan.)

The late Archbishop Daeger, of Santa Fe, New Mexico, just before his tragic death, told me what he thought of William Jennings Bryan. He said "I lived near Mr. Bryan in Lincoln, Nebraska. He was a great Christian, a thoroughly sincere man. I wish we had more people like him."

Once I met Bryan in New Mexico. He displayed a great paternal instinct to talk to me about his son. He seemed exceedingly proud of the Southwest, and he showed the greatest pleasure in discussing the studies of his son at the University of Arizona, located in Tucson. He said he stopped over in Albuquerque for the simple reason he wished to go to Tucson to see his son. I gathered that the great city of Albuquerque would not have enjoyed his lovely discourse if it hadn't been for the University at Tucson. Bryan expected his son to become a great lawyer.

Bryan visited Santa Fe. I always think this is a gorgeous story which I narrated to various people, including presidents of railroads, famous financiers and writers. The last time I told the story it was to George Horace Lorimer, editor of the *Saturday Evening Post,* and to its able financial writer, Garret Garet. This is the story: The speaker is J. S. Candelario, owner of the unique curio shop of America. Candelario said, "Of course I know Bryan. He buys all his Indian blankets here. He's a big Democrat. I like him. Everybody comes to my store. Theodore Roosevelt was one of my visitors. Great people are known to me. Bryan called here. He wanted to see me. Of course I had to show him the bells. I rang the bells for Bryan. Bryan had just toured the world. He listened attentively to my ringing of the bells. Then he looked at the dates above the bells. I wanted to give Bryan a good time. I said to him "The first bell you heard ringing, Mr. Bryan, is dated as you see, 1480. The second bell is 1340." I thought Bryan would be impressed. He was not. He paused, and then in that rich voice of his he said "Do I understand these are the oldest bells in the world?" "I think they are," said Candelario. "Well," said Bryan, "In my travels around the world, I think I've seen older bells."

"Where?" asked Candelario.

"I think in Moscow."

Mr. Candelario said "Mr. Bryan, you don't read the inscription right. That figure isn't A.D. It's *before* Christ."

Bryan remarked to his guide "This is a priceless curio store."

Candelario was so impressed with Bryan—especially as Bryan was the great Democrat—that he then showed him a suit of clothes worn by a man who was struck by lightning. The odd feature of the suit of clothes was, they didn't show any effects of lightning. Bryan chuckled. Candelario's next possession, which he showed in progressive order, was a silver spur worn by the Emperor Maximilian about the time he was executed. The spur bore a crest with a large letter "A." It was kept in a huge vault and never shown except to distinguished people.

Bryan considered Santa Fe the City Unique, Candelario the prize curio collector of the world. Bryan intimated that it was the joy of his life to visit this ancient city.

The last time Bryan was in Santa Fe was in 1918, and strange to say, his voice lacked that wonderful clarity which made him world famous as an orator. One of his greatest admirers, hearing Bryan's oration, remarked, "Something has come over his voice. Certainly it isn't whiskey. Bryan never took a drink in his life. Certainly it isn't old age. The man's mind is as clear as a bell. What has come over Bryan?"

I replied, "Disappointment."

Bryan had the stolid indifference to criticism which is worthy of a great man. According to newspaper reporters whom I have met, Bryan faced bravely the election returns on his first and second defeat, but the third seemed to get him down. According to one reporter Bryan remarked, in the night of the third defeat, "I have nothing to say. I feel tired." The reporter said "Bryan is the only human being in the world who never felt fatigued."

A lot of people said that Bryan overate. I never saw Bryan eat but one meal in my life. It was at a banquet. He didn't eat any more than anyone else. He did not call for a second helping.

Bryan knew the secret of repose. When others were worrying about the outcome of his campaigns; when others were tempted to take a snort of whiskey to pep up their jaded nerves, Bryan sought and found slumber. Bryan knew the art of power through repose. He had a splendid physique. He had been brought up on the farm. He required no stimulants whatsoever. Tobacco and alcohol were unknown to him. He told me that quiet and fresh air rejuvenated him after an arduous journey.

Bryan made a tremendous hit with the late President William H. Taft—according to a friend of Mr. Taft—by his sincerity and boyish simplicity. I think it was in the campaign of 1912 that he talked to ex-President Taft in a dining room when they happened to be at the same hotel. According to reports, Bryan said to Taft "Hope you don't mind what I'm saying about you in this campaign. I have said much worse against Theodore Roosevelt." Taft used his usual gesture, pummeled the linen covered table with his soft, graceful hands, and replied "I think it's awfully nice of you."

I once delivered a message to Theodore Roosevelt down in San Diego, California. Roosevelt told me what he thought of certain politicians, and he seemed extremely annoyed about the response he was getting with his Progressive movement. Bryan had just been in San Diego. As a great admirer of Bryan I thought I would mention the great Commoner to Theodore Roosevelt, but five minutes before, a newspaper was delivered to my hands with an interview with

Theodore Roosevelt on Willian Jennings Bryan. It seems that Mr. Roosevelt had been ruder than ex-President Taft, and said something to the effect that Bryan's discourses resembled oceans of mush.

One of my friends, a newspaper reporter for Hearst, told me that he interviewed William J. Bryan when Bryan was Secretary of State, and that Bryan was most courteous, and gave him a marvelous story about a great wave of peace sweeping the United States. Unfortunately this interviewer sent out a dispatch to the *Santa Fe New Mexican,* about the great wave of peace, and it came over the wires "The great dove of peace." According to reports, Mr. Bryan was not flattered by the change of the word "wave" into "dove," and there are rumors that he made unkind remarks about the inaccuracy of newspaper reporters.

One time in his life Mr. Bryan was very cautious with newspaper reporters, asked them to write their interviews with him on a typewriter in his office in Lincoln, Nebraska, and submit the copy to him. He never did that with me, but when I interviewed him, he wasn't running for president.

Newspaper men loved Bryan because he was so courteous. If he was pressed for time, you'd never know it.

I thought the world of Bryan, and I told Opie Read, famous novelist, about my feeling. Read, tall, stately, wearing a black coat like Bryan wore—a sort of Abe Lincoln costume—showed annoyance over my enthusiasm about Bryan. Read said he called on Bryan, gave Bryan a lecture on the importance of preparedness, told Bryan that if the Germans struck him in the face, he would pull out a gun to defend himself—said a lot of other things. Read said that Bryan replied "Don't get personal."

Read discussed Bryan and other political leaders, remarking "After all, a politician is different."

Bryan loved Indian blankets, and bought them in Santa Fe, New Mexico. According to Candelario, he ordered 22 at one time. They were for his house in Miami. Bryan undoubtedly had a feeling for color, design and Indian art.

A SUGGESTED SENTIMENT.

Dear Mr. ——

I lack time for an interview, but if we can compromise on a Thanksgiving Sentiment, take your pencil & I will dictate it. Thus:

A few days ago one of the interviewers offered to let me do a "Thanksgiving Sentiment." I was not able to take advantage of the opportunity, for I had already declined two chances, & it would not be fair to be inconsistent & unreliable unless I could do good by it or there was graft in it somewhere, for the family.

Mark Twain's note to Dunne, showing that the beginning of the "Sentiment" was cut off from the page

APPENDIX 4

An Interview with Mark Twain?

[THE FOLLOWING "INTERVIEW" appeared on the front page of the *Times* of Washington, D.C., on November 27, 1905. It became known in journalistic circles as an interview which, having been solicited by Brian Bōrú Dunne, was actually written or dictated by Mark Twain himself. The piece is not in the form of an interview, however, and since Dunne's name is never mentioned, his own part in the project was not evident to the readers. The main section of it appears to be an essay by Twain, accompanied by "autographic sentiments," consisting of a little more than a paragraph from the essay, evidently in Twain's handwriting. These are followed by a largely unrelated and unsigned news story headlined "Mark Twain Here; / Will See President," giving some details of the popular writer's social activities in Washington, D.C., and his intention to leave town that same afternoon. This item was very clearly written by Dunne, who cleverly insinuated into it a brief and somewhat disconnected comment on the essay. Twain, he wrote, did not care to "talk for publication," but wanted to "play the role of 'dictator,' and what he dictated precedes." Twain edited his own manuscript, said Dunne, "and wrote at the head of it in small capitals 'A SUGGESTED SENTIMENT.'"

An interview with a celebrated humorist which turned into a dictated essay was doubtless the kind of amusing story which Dunne would share with his colleagues, and even perpetuate among his friends. Some time later, it even got into his dossier. In an undated letter "To Whom It May Concern," Frank P. Morse, former Sunday editor of the *Times,* wrote that Dunne "was the only Washington newspaper man who succeeded in extracting an interview (self-written) from Mark Twain." Although Dunne's name was not publicly associated with this "interview," then, his role in the enterprise was known and even circulated among some journalists. Remarkably, however, the whole *Times* article has been passed over by most Twain scholars ever since. At least it is not noticed by Louis J. Budd in his listing of interviews with Mark Twain. Fortunately, we are able to resurrect it here through the efforts of Brian Boru II, who in searching through his father's papers discovered a number of documents which enable us to trace part of its history. In the transmission, of course, the tale would become legendary as well as amusing, and it would retain the identity of an intended interview as part of the inherent humor. One of our earlier records of it occurs in a letter to Dunne written in 1942 by George Hiram Brownell, Secretary-Treasurer of the newly formed Mark Twain Association of America, and editor of their small monthly journal, *The Twainian.* George Ade, another popular humorist who had been a friend of Twain's, was the president of the association, and on November 5 Brownell told Dunne that he had read a letter to Ade in which "you mention that you once wrote a story of your interview with Mark Twain for the Washington *Times*—or, rather, that Twain wrote the interview for you." The distinction between a story and an interview is already blurred here, and it gets even more obscured when Brownell asks Dunne for "the date on which this interview story was published in the *Times.*" Was it an interview, a story, or an interview story? But Brownell intended to write an article "about this interview," and asked Dunne which portion of "the published article is still in existence in your hands in manuscript form?"

Three weeks later, on November 23, Brownell thanked Dunne for having sent on "a large envelope," but the problem which seems to have been cleared up for him is not at all resolved for us. In this letter, Brownell speaks of the coincidence that he already had in his files a photostat of "the *Times* story, written by Twain as a self-interview," but had had "no knowledge of the identity of the 'interviewer' mentioned in the first line of the Twain story." And he asks whether Dunne would mind his "making a little mention of the contents of your letter in our December issue." Yet in his article, which appeared in that issue, Brownell says nothing at all about Dunne. Instead he quotes from an article written for the *Miami News* by George Ade, to whom Brownell had sent his photostats. Ade quoted about half of Twain's *Times* article, and Brownell repeated that in the *Twainian*. But there it died. In 1942, so great was the demand for space for war news that Ade's article was not picked up by the Associated Press, as it was meant to be, and, in Brownell's words, "Ade's story appears to have delighted only the comparatively limited number of readers of the *News* in the Miami area." And, of course, to the two hundred readers of *The Twainian.* But even that printing seems to have gone unnoticed by Twain scholars.

The whole problem ought to have been resolved by a simple reading of the story as it appeared in the *Times,* but that too is oddly ambiguous, and to the present editors the issue was made even more complicated by two notes, assumed to be in Twain's handwriting, which Brian Boru II found among his father's papers. The first is a fragment addressed to Dunne, but the rather cramped writing seems to have been squeezed into a small space at the top of a page, from which it has been cut off:

A SUGGESTED SENTIMENT

Dear Mr. Dunne=

I lack time for an interview, but if we can compromise on a Thanksgiving Sentiment, take your pencil & I will dictate it. Thus:

At first, then, it would appear that the redoubtable Dunne, whom Frank Morse once described as "the most successful interviewer in the Nation's Capital," having been denied a full interview, was eloquent enough to persuade the famous humorist to contribute *something* to the newspaper. Perhaps they discussed the arrangement which Dunne described in an interview six months later with John Temple Graves, Independent candidate for vice-president, whom he compared to Twain: "Like the world's greatest humorist, Col. Graves prefers to dictate what he has to say, or plays reporter himself and writes down his answers to questions furnished him." At any rate, since Dunne and Twain, each with a powerful sense of humor, met together in the convivial atmosphere of Twain's hotel, the proposed "Sentiment" must have evolved in some way into a statement which, with some imaginative wit, they could regard as an interview without the interviewer, or even a "self-written" interview—with the journalist mentioned only in the first paragraph. A personal note offering to dictate it would at least bring the interviewer into the picture.

The other note in Twain's hand is on a small sheet of paper, unsigned, with a typed description on the back of it: "Part of MS. written by Mark Twain for Brian Ború Dunne, Sunday afternoon, November 26, 1905, at the New Willard Hotel, Washington, D.C.":

> A few days ago one of the interviewers [Dunne] offered to let me do a Thanksgiving Sentiment. I was not able to take advantage of the opportunity, for I had already declined two chances, & it would not be fair to be inconsistent & unreliable unless I could do good by it or there was graft in it somewhere, for the family.

Without knowing the situation, a reader might wonder here why an interviewer would ask for a "sentiment," but that was Dunne's predicament exactly, and since this note formed the first paragraph of the printed piece, clearly it was meant to be published. In spite of the comic reference to graft, only Twain and Dunne would see the humor. If the notion of calling the rest of the printed piece a "self-interview" was perhaps Twain's idea, Dunne could well conceive of it as a "substitute" interview, with of course all traces of the interviewer conveniently deleted.

But since the editors of this volume had little knowledge of Mark Twain's habits or of his handwriting, it seemed appropriate to consult Mr. Robert H. Hirst, the General Editor of the Mark Twain Project at the University of California at Berkeley. It seems that the two notes printed above are indeed in Mark Twain's handwriting, but the "Autographic Sentiments" reproduced in the *Times* are not. That piece is almost certainly in the hand of Isabel V. Lyon, Twain's secretary at the time, who did not, however, accompany him to Washington. The story that can be pieced together from all the known facts is necessarily speculative in part, but with the indispensable help of Robert Hirst and Brian Boru Dunne II we can offer an account that seems at least plausible, and to us compelling. Twain had recently sat for a quite different interview and "sentiment," which appeared in the *New York World* on November 26 and was to be printed in sixty-two western newspapers on the 30th, which was Thanksgiving Day and by coincidence Twain's seventieth birthday. During his few days in Washington, his time was indeed short, taken up mostly with social activities, ending with a visit to President Theodore Roosevelt. When Twain says that he had already declined two "offers," he undoubtedly meant two interviewers in the Washington area. But it is not implausible that he had with him a text dictated to his secretary before he left home, and that its very presence solved the problem of what to offer or to adapt for the ardently persuasive Dunne to publish. The piece itself, or extracts from it, could at least serve as a "Thanksgiving Sentiment." And yet, as we have pointed out, the first paragraph of the printed version was written specifically for Dunne as an introduction, and so could not be included in the "autographic sentiment" because it was truly in Twain's own handwriting, not that of his secretary. In fact, Brian Boru II discovered that the contour of the bottom edge of the short note fits exactly the top contour of the longer one. The two were therefore written at the same time, the cramped handwriting of the shorter note reflecting the lack of space and perhaps even the "conviviality" of a Sunday afternoon in a Washington hotel. As to Twain's offer to "dictate" it to Dunne, Mr. Hirst offers the information that, when deciding to insert items into his autobiography, Twain was not known for strictly observing the distinction between what he wrote and what he literally dictated. Dunne, however, perhaps in a sober moment of reflection on the Spirit of Truth, must have declined to carry the joke about Twain's dictation into print, and so he separated the short note from the longer one. An "insider," however, can see how certain remnants of the joke did, after all, get into the descriptive story which Dunne printed just below Twain's, and Dunne must have explained that to Ade and to Brownell. The famed humorist did, in fact, play something like the role of "dictator" in setting the terms for this "interview," and as to the manuscript, all Dunne had to say truly was that it had been dictated—though not to him. When he says that Twain "edited his own manuscript," however, he is providing a clue to the reader and perhaps even to future editors, though we may doubt that he had the present editors in mind. The document he refers to is the one which Twain had dictated to his secretary, as can be seen from his own corrections on that part of it published as a facsimile "autograph." In view of the fierce journalistic competition in Washington at that time, the era of yellow journalism and newspaper wars, the exceptional feat which Dunne had accomplished lay in putting together an exclusive Twain original for the *Times*, whether it be called a story, an interview, an interview story, a self-interview, a sentiment, or just an original essay, dictated or not. The real joke, of course, was on the *Times*, for printing a fake autograph. That must have been especially amusing to the two "conspirators," one of them a "dictator" to boot. And since this Mark Twain Original has managed to elude scholarly notice for so many decades, we are happy to print the piece here so that it can at last be entered into the Twain canon.]

Less Cause for Thanks
Than Man Has His God

Expresses This Opinion, Pointing
to the Massacres in Russia and the
Life Insurance Scandals in America.

By Mark Twain

A few days ago one of the interviewers offered to let me do a Thanksgiving sentiment. I was not able to take advantage of the opportunity for I had already declined two chances and it would not be fair to be inconsistent and unreliable unless I could do good by it or there was graft in it somewhere, for the family.

Besides there is another aspect to this matter. Every year every person in America concentrates all his thought upon one thing, the cataloguing of his reasons for being thankful to the Deity for the blessings conferred upon him and upon the human race during the expiring twelve months. This is well and as it should be; but it is too one-sided. No one ever seems to think of the Deity's side of it; apparently no one concerns himself to inquire how much or how little He has had to be thankful for during the same period; apparently no one has had good feeling enough to wish He might have a thanksgiving day, too. There is nothing right about this.

Is Everything Satisfactory to Him?

Do you suppose everything has gone to His satisfaction during the year? Do you believe He is as sweepingly thankful as our nation is going to be, as indicated by the enthusiasms which will appear in the papers on the thirtieth of this month from the pens of the distinguished persons appointed to phrase its thankfulness on that day?

We may be unstintedly thankful but can that be really the case with Him? If He had a voice how would He regard the year's results in Russia? What would He be thankful for there? The servants of that government, in patriotic obedience to its commands, have lately killed and wounded 50,000 Jews by unusual and unpleasant methods, butchering the men and the women with knife and bayonet; flinging them out of windows; saturating them with kerosene, and setting fire to them; shutting them up in cellars and smothering them with smoke; drenching children with boiling water; tearing other children asunder by the methods of the Middle Ages. Doubtless the most that He can be thankful for is that the carnage and the suffering are not as bad as they might have been.

Life Insurance Tolerably Rotten.

He will have noticed that life insurance in New York has gone tolerably rotten, and that the widow and the orphan have had a sorrowful time of it at the hands of their chosen protectors. Doubtless, the most that He is thankful for is that the rottenness and the robberies have not been absolutely complete. He has noticed that the political smell ascending from New York, Philadelphia and sixty or seventy other municipalities has been modified a little—temporarily—and is doubtless thankful for that transient reprieve.

He has observed that King Leopold's destruction of innocent life in the Congo is not as great this year as it was last, by as much as 100,000 victims, because of diminishing material; he has also noticed that America and other great powers—accessories before the fact and responsible for these murders, especially America—are properly thankful on our Thanksgiving Day and for nineteen previous Thanksgiving Days; and without doubt He is himself thankful that matters in the Congo are not as irretrievably bad as they might be, and that some of the natives are still left alive.

Not as Rosy as Ours.

One is justified in fearing that the Deity's Thanksgiving Day is not as rosy as ours will appear when the Thanksgiving sentiments blossom out in our journals and that if He, now voiceless, should utter a sentiment it would be tinged with a pathetic regret.

Mark Twain Here;
Will See President

Samuel Clemens arrived in Washington Saturday night accompanied by Col. George M. Harvey and H. E. Bowen, both of New York. They will return to New York this afternoon, it is said, after the distinguished writer has had an opportunity to meet President Roosevelt.

During the short time he has been in the city, Mark Twain's wakeful hours have been mostly taken up with social engagements. A few hours after his arrival Saturday night he was given a dinner at the Willard by Colonel Harvey, the guests including Secretary Root, Secretary Taft, and Wayne MacVeagh.

Wished to Dictate.

Mr. Clemens did not care to talk for publication unless he could play the role of "dictator," and what he dictated precedes. He edited his own manuscript, and wrote at the head of it in small capitals "A SUGGESTED SENTIMENT."

Within three days of rounding out three score and ten, Mark Twain appeared at the Willard hotel today to have within him the "arteries of a man of forty." His lithe step, his erect carriage, his clear complexion, his piercing hazel eyes, his deep clear voice, all these characteristics combined would make the average man think Mark Twain to be merely perpetrating one of his jokes when he tells us that he will celebrate his seventieth anniversary this Thanksgiving Day.

BIBLIOGRAPHY OF WORKS CITED

Badolato, Francesco, "Meeting Dr. Sculco's Son," *Gissing Newsletter* 10, no. 3, July 1974, pp. 7–8.

Bainville, Jacques, *Napoléon*, trans. Hamish Miles (Boston: Little, Brown, 1933).

Baugh, Alfred C., ed., *A Literary History of England* (New York: Appleton-Century-Crofts, 1948).

Bertz, Eduard, *Philosophie des Fahrrads* (Leipzig: Reissner, 1900).

Call, Annie Payson, *Power through Repose* (Boston: Roberts Bros., 1891).

Carlyle, Thomas, *On Heroes and Hero-Worship* (London: James Fraser, 1841).

Dunne, Brian Ború, *Cured! The 70 Adventures of a Dyspeptic* (Philadelphia: John C. Winston, 1914 and 1937).

Forster, John, *The Life of Charles Dickens* (London: Chapman and Hall, 1872–74).

Freudenthal, Elsbeth, *Flight into History* (Norman: University of Oklahoma Press, 1949).

Gettmann, Royal, ed., *George Gissing and H. G. Wells* (London: Rupert Hart-Davis, 1961).

Gibbons, James, Cardinal, *The Faith of Our Fathers* (Baltimore: Murphy; London: P. Washbourne, 1877).

Gouin, François, *L'Art d'enseigner et d'étudier les langues* (Paris: G. Fischbasher, 1880), trans. Howard Swan and Victor Bétis as *The Art of Teaching and Studying Languages* (London: Philip, 1892).

Gould, George Milbry, *Biographic Clinics* (Philadelphia: P. Blakiston, 6 vols., 1903–1909). *Concerning Lafcadio Hearn* (London: T. F. Unwin; Philadelphia: G. W. Jacobs, 1908). *Suggestions to Medical Writers* (Philadelphia: Medical Publishing Co., 1901).

Gould, George Milbry, and Pyle, Walter Lytle, *A Compend of the Diseases of the Eye* (Baltimore, 1899). *Cyclopedia of Practical Medicine and Surgery* (Philadelphia: P. Blakiston, 1900).

Grylls, David, "The Annual Return to Old Grub Street: What Samuel Johnson Meant to Gissing," *Gissing Newsletter* 20, no. 1, January 1984, pp. 1–27.

Lanciani, Rodolfo Amadeo, *Ancient Rome in the Light of Recent Discoveries* (London: Macmillan, 1888). *Pagan and Christian Rome* (London: Macmillan, 1892).

Lowitt, Richard, *Bronson M. Cutting: Progressive Politician* (Albuquerque: University of New Mexico Press, 1992).

Martin, Georges, *Histoire et généalogie de la Maison de Croÿ* (Privately printed: La Ricamarie, France, 1980).

McCarthy, Justin Huntly, *A Short History of the United States* (London: Hodder & Stoughton, 1898; Chicago and New York: H. S. Stone, 1899).

Muller, Herbert J., *Modern Fiction: A Study of Values* (New York and London: Funk and Wagnall, 1937).

Murger, Henri, *Scènes de la vie de Bohème* (Paris, 1847–49).

Nelson, Walter Henry, *The Soldier Kings: The House of Hohenzollern* (New York: Putnam's Sons, 1970).

Pemble, John, *The Mediterranean Passion* (Oxford: Clarendon Press; New York: Oxford University Press, 1987).

Roberts, Morley, *The Private Life of Henry Maitland* (London: E. Nash, 1912).

Scott, Sir Walter, *Life of Napoleon Buonaparte,* in *Prose Works of Sir Walter Scott* (Edinburgh: Robert Cadell, 1835).

Selig, Robert L., *George Gissing: Lost Stories from America* (Lewiston, N.Y.: Edwin Mellen Press, 1992).

Shipley, Neal R., "'The Constant Question of Finances': The Ordeal of F. Marion Crawford," *University of Mississippi Studies in English,* n.s. 6, 1988.

Ward, Adolphus William, *Dickens* (London: Macmillan, "English Men of Letters Series," 1882).

Wells, H. G., *Experiment in Autobiography* (New York: Macmillan, 1934). "The Liberal Fear of Russia," *Harper's Magazine,* September 19, 1914, pp. 268–70.

"C.3.3." [Wilde, Oscar], *The Ballad of Reading Gaol* (London: Leonard Smithers, Royal Arcade, 1898).

INDEX OF NAMES. TITLES, AND MISCELLANEA

Rampolla, Mariano, Cardinal, 68, 88, 146
Reynaert, Honoré-Arthur, 69, 88
Richardson, Benjamin Ward, 4
Roberts, Morley, 5, 6, 8, 10, 133, 138. *The Private Life of Henry Maitland,* 133, 137, 138
Rockefeller, John D., 32, 169
Roosevelt, Theodore, 29, 32, 167
Ruggles of Red Gap (Harry Leon Wilson), 14, 56, 83–84

San Antonio Colony, 15, 16, 22, 76
Santa Fe New Mexican, 30, 31
Scott, Miss E. T., 75
Scott, Robert, 143, 149–50
Scott, Sir Walter, *Life of Napoleon Buonaparte,* 85, 115, 123, 129
Sculco, Dr. Riccardo, of Cotrone, 63, 87, 120, 142
Selig, Robert L., *George Gissing: Lost Stories from America,* 112
Shakespeare, William, 52, 77, 98, 164
Sharp, William, 4
Shaw, George Bernard, 24, 169. *The Doctors' Delusion,* 24
Shorter, Clement King, 4, 5, 9
Shortridge, John Wood, 52, 82, 98, 109, 116, 126, 143
Siringo, Charley, 32, 169
Smith, George, 152
Stead, W. T., 147
"Stella," 60, 140, 144
Stonor, Bishop Edmund, 145, 152
Sturmer, H. H., 11, 75, 86
Swinnerton, Frank, 88
Swinton-Hunter, Robert Hepburne, 86

Tacchi, Dr. Ilario, 58, 85, 146, 155–56
Thackeray, W. M., 151. *Vanity Fair,* 134, 143, 151
Thornycroft, Hamo, 5
Times (London), 35, 36, 37, 100, 117
Times Literary Supplement, 36
Travers family, 5, 75
Tribuna, 58, 83, 121
Tribune (Bainbridge, Georgia), 28

Triple Alliance, 57, 85, 123, 124, 130, 142
Trollope, Mrs. Frances, 108, 112
Turgenev, Ivan, 76
Twain, Mark, 22, 24, 27, 29, 32, 37, 166, 190–99

Umberto, King of Italy, 33, 58, 59, 65, 85–86, 122, 124, 127, 129, 145.

Vaughan, Herbert Alfred, Cardinal, 144, 152
Vergil, 111
Verne, Jules, 61
Victor Emmanuel III, King of Italy, 122, 128
Vestnik Evropy, 76

Walker, Dr. Jane, 87
Ward, Adolphus William, 12
Ward, Justine, 30, 170
Washington, D. C., *Times,* 16, 22, 29, 113, 162, 166, 191
Wells, H. G., 1, 2, 3, 4, 5, 10, 14, 18, 19, 20, 23, 24, 29, 32, 33, 34, 35, 36, 37, 41, 46, 47, 80–81, 87, 93, 100, 103, 110, 111, 112–13, 130, 131, 133, 134–35, 136, 138, 139, 141, 145, 146, 151, 153, 154, 163, 164, 168, 170. *Experiment in Autobiography,* 1, 35, 36, 81, 111, 112. "The Liberal Fear of Russia," 135, 138, 139. *The War That Will End War,* 139. Mrs. Wells, 10, 18, 134, 136
Whale, George, 5
Wilde, Oscar, 117, 126
William II, Emperor of Germany, 17, 71, 124, 128, 129, 130, 146, 156–57, 167–68
Willis, John, 32
Wright, Wilbur and Orville, 27, 32, 164

Zangwill, Israel, 5
Zola, Emile, 146, 156

SUBJECT INDEX
OF THE MEMOIRS